HOW NOT TO F**K UP PIP

The step-by-step guide to completing your claim

CHARLIE ANDERSON

Rethink

First published in Great Britain in 2026
by Rethink Press (www.rethinkpress.com)

Back cover photography by www.thesoulofmylens.co.uk

Disclaimer

This book provides general information and guidance on applying for Personal Independence Payment (PIP) and Adult Disability Payment (ADP) based on the author's personal experience and research. It does not constitute legal or medical advice, and no guarantee is made regarding outcomes. Readers should seek advice from qualified professionals where appropriate.

This book is dedicated to every one of us living with a disability or chronic illness. Our world is not disabled friendly… yet! There is no manual about adapting to the limits we face, no training for surviving the daily experience of going through this hell. Many of you reading this will be in what I call 'survival mode' – fighting through every minute of the day just to make it to the next. I'm sorry.

Chronic illness changes our lives forever, but your life is not over. It's just going to be different from what you were anticipating. You can adapt and you will eventually thrive (OK, maybe in a chronically ill kind of way… but still, thrive!).

Remember: you are a warrior. You are stubborn as fuck. This book is for you. You can do this.

Contents

Introduction: PIP And ADP

If you're reading this book, you're probably overwhelmed, exhausted or just plain fed up. You're trying to apply for PIP (Personal Independence Payment) or ADP (Adult Disability Payment), and you've realised it's not 'just a form', it's a full-blown emotional battle. This book is here to guide you through it.

Whether you live in England, Wales, Northern Ireland or Scotland, this guide applies to you. Throughout the book, I will just refer to 'PIP', because while the forms differ and departments may vary (Department for Work and Pensions (DWP), Department for Communities (DfC), Social Security Scotland), the guidance is the same. They assess us all in the same way so what you need to know to win is the same.

This book is focused on PIP claims, but everything here can be used for all stages of the process, be it, your Review, Change of Circumstance, Mandatory Reconsideration or Tribunal.

Please work through this book systematically. You cannot skip bits! Think of applying for PIP like trying to do a 10,000-piece jigsaw, but pieces are missing and others belong to a completely different puzzle. It can be frustrating, time-consuming and emotionally draining, but by following all the steps in this book, you will be able to:

- Face the reality of your life
- Learn the facts about PIP
- Focus on what's relevant
- Complete your form
- Prepare your evidence document
- Be ready for the assessment
- Understand the next steps

If you do not have the time, energy or willpower to follow this book step by step, don't panic. You can save yourself months of stress by just booking the PIP entitlement assessment I offer, or a consultancy meeting, where we get literally *everything done in one session*. To book help, scan the QR code below or visit: https://calendly.com/charliesjourney.

The accompanying workbook

This is a really good moment to download your free workbook, available at https://charlies-journey.co.uk. In your workbook, you will find:

- A space to record your top three conditions
- Your daily activity diary
- A list of the 12 activities that PIP assesses
- Details of the points system
- Key questions to guide your answers
- The evidence template
- 2 blank claim forms
- 2 blank practice notes (for assessment prep)

You will need to make notes in your workbook as we go through this book, and these notes will then form the basis of your PIP journey. As we work through the book, I will be encouraging you to make notes, reflect honestly on your daily challenges and follow step-by-step instructions. By the end, you'll have identified your PIP scores, gathered key evidence, completed your form or written your PIP document, and built a practical action plan. Remember: this is *your* life, *your* claim and you are *unique*.

My story and how I got good at PIP

This bit of the book will not help you complete your PIP form, so if you're in a rush, feel free to skip it. I am including it because context matters. If you're going to trust me to guide you through one of the most exhausting, bureaucratic nightmares of your life, you deserve to understand who I am, what my background is and why I'm good at this.

You can check out my LinkedIn, website, client reviews and YouTube comments. Fair warning: Newspapers tend not to be too complimentary when writing about what I do. I don't fit their mould, and I'm fine with that.

Let me introduce myself. Hi, I'm Charlie. I've lived with severe psoriasis since I was a young child. My skin would crack, bleed and shed constantly. It looked and felt horrendous. Here's me at 15 years old, when my psoriasis was pretty good.

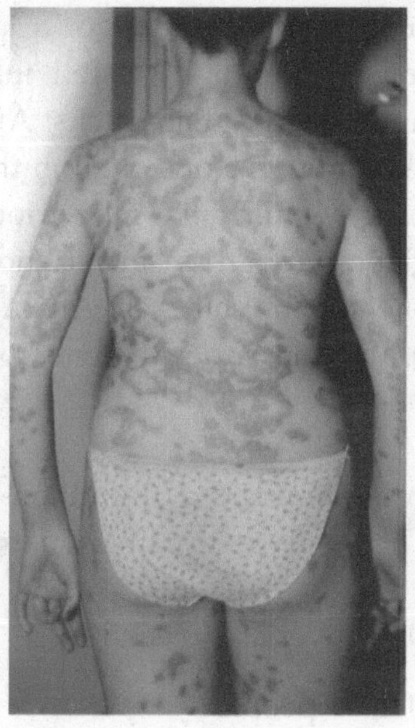

Living with a chronic illness, specifically psoriasis, defined me. It taught me early on how brutal the world could be. I was severely bullied, and my survival strategy was simple: push people away before they could hurt me.

As a child, my one big dream was travelling to and working in Africa. When I was 16, I tried to join the army, but I was turned down because of my psoriasis. I fell into nursing, imagining myself in A&E or even a war zone overseas, but MRSA and psoriasis swiftly ended that career before it even began. Still, in that same year (1998), I made it to Namibia, and I knew instantly that Africa was my home. Back in the UK, I was lost. Once again, I was without a career.

I ended up in Weymouth and got a job in a New Look warehouse. Eventually, I fell into transport, thinking, 'The Red Cross has trucks! Africa here we come!' I worked my arse off to climb the ranks so a reputable charity would take me seriously. I joined Clipper Logistics and Transaid (whose motto is 'Transport for Life'), travelling to Africa twice a year. Everyone around me supported my plan to move there full-time.

In the UK, I was running a multimillion-pound transport contract across five sites. I was managing:

- Over 1,000 deliveries a week
- A team of 200+ people
- Strategic planning, health and safety, HR, training and development
- A team culture rooted in prioritising people, driven by the belief that failure is not an option

With Transaid, I worked with local teams on transport projects that literally saved lives! Life was amazing. I was finally achieving my dreams.

Then, in 2007, aged 29, everything changed once again. I got sick and was diagnosed with psoriatic arthritis. Within two years, I couldn't even put my own socks on. I gained over two stone and lost my thirties to the disease and the side effects of treatment.

I lost Africa. I lost the chance of becoming a mother. I lived in constant panic: how was I going to survive, both financially and mentally?

Eventually, I found out about PIP. I applied, knowing nothing. It was horrendous. I full-on snot-sobbed just doing the form. Being scarred by the PIP process made me furious. That fury became fuel. I learnt everything that I could about the PIP process and became determined to help others. I started my YouTube channel when I was 45 (you know, the perfect age to become a YouTuber!) because I did not want anyone to lose a decade of their life as I had. I also knew I was about to lose another career to my health, which happened in 2023.

Once again, I found myself without a job, but I believe everything happens for a reason. Suddenly, my 'How to do a PIP Claim' video took off, and I realised there was something that I could do. Something that needed doing. I quickly became so busy that I started my consultancy, helping others to navigate the PIP system and get what they deserve. Eventually, my knowledge and experience gained from working with clients across all types of chronic illnesses led me to write this book. It is so important to me that I contribute to people's lives in a positive manner, and this book is my way of trying to do that. But it is also a part of trying to pay my mortgage and afford food when I am not fit for 'normal' work.

My plan is to review and update this book every year or so. For those of you truly impacted by severe chronic illness: I want you to win. I want you to know I'm reputable. You can trust what I say, and when I fuck up, I promise I'll tell you.

I hope this helps you understand a bit about me so that you feel more comfortable following my guidance. You may also want to read the author biography at the end of the book, where I include some real stats and facts to back up what I have said.

Charlie xx

PS – My end goal is to improve people's quality of life. Successfully claiming PIP is just the beginning. Together, we will help you soar!

PART ONE
UNDERSTANDING PIP

1
What Is PIP?

Personal Independence Payment (PIP) is a type of government funding for people living with chronic illness or a disability that affects their ability to carry out everyday tasks. It is designed to help you stay independent by providing support towards the extra living costs we face, because living with chronic illness is expensive.

You'll notice I use the terms 'chronic illness' and 'disability' pretty interchangeably throughout this book. That's not because they mean the same thing to everyone, far from it. Some people who are chronically ill don't see themselves as disabled. Others who are disabled wouldn't describe themselves as ill or even 'different'. Many people feel they don't fit neatly into either box.

Language in this space is messy, emotional and deeply personal. I've done my best to keep things broad and inclusive but I'm not trying to pin down anyone's identity. I want to help, and this book is for you.

PIP is not means-tested. This means it doesn't depend on your income or savings, it doesn't affect other benefits, and you can spend it on whatever you want.

How PIP is structured

PIP has two sections:

- **Daily Living:** Covers 10 everyday activities (eg washing, dressing, preparing food)
- **Mobility:** Covers two activities (planning and following journeys, moving around)

Each section has two levels of funding:

- **8–11 points:** Lower rate (sometimes referred to as 'standard')
- **12+ points:** Higher rate (sometimes referred to as 'enhanced')

As of writing, the weekly payment rates are as follows:

Section	Lower rate	Higher rate
Daily Living	£76.70	£114.60
Mobility	£30.30	£80.00

Check www.gov.uk/pip for current rates.

You are paid every four weeks, and your award letter will confirm when payments start and your award length.

Motability cars

If you're awarded the enhanced rate of the mobility section, you have a choice: you can either take the money as part of your benefits payments or you can use it to lease a new car through the Motability Scheme. For some, it's life-changing, particularly if you need a wheelchair-accessible vehicle (WAV) or specific modifications to either drive or travel in the vehicle.

My advice? Think carefully before choosing the car. It can make people jealous of your shiny new vehicle, and sadly, that can sometimes be enough to lead someone to report you to the DWP because they do not 'believe' you're ill enough to qualify.

How PIP works in practice

PIP is supposed to help us live independently, but in reality, it often feels like it's designed to break us. Everything about this process is strategic, and let's be honest, the goal is to save the government money. That's why you'll face:

- Loads of paperwork
- Long, uncertain waits
- Errors in reports
- Unfair or inaccurate point scoring
- Stressful appeals

At times, it can feel like you're being forced to prove you are not a liar. Many people fail, not because they aren't entitled, but because they focus on areas that PIP isn't interested in. I firmly believe that if you stand your ground and follow the guidance in this book, you *will* be treated fairly in the end.

PIP is not about what you *used* to be able to do or what you *could* do if you push yourself and then suffer more. It's about your current daily life – what you actually do *now*, on both bad and better days.

Assessors compare us to able-bodied people and ask:

- Are you **Safe**?
- Are you **Consistent**?
- **And** are you **Reliable**?

That's SCAR, like the bad lion in *The Lion King*.

PIP is a nightmare, but it's worth it! It opens doors and can massively improve your quality of life, financially, practically and emotionally.

Who can claim PIP?

Does your chronic illness significantly impact your daily life? If so, you might be eligible for PIP.

The basic eligibility rules are:

- Your condition must have lasted at least three months and be expected to continue for at least another nine months.
- You must be over 16 and under state pension age when you first apply.
- You must live in the UK (with some exceptions for people in the armed forces or living abroad – check www.gov.uk/pip for details).

It's that simple! Well, sort of… I mean, if it were that simple, there would be no reason to write this book!

Here's a list of things people worry about, but none of these affect your eligibility:

- Owning property
- Working part-time or full-time
- Being self-employed or running your own business
- Having a partner with a good income
- Having savings
- Receiving other benefits
- Living in rented accommodation
- Having children (whether they live with you or not)
- Receiving child-related benefits
- Taking medication or receiving treatment
- Having a condition that *might* be cured
- Having a condition that will last the rest of your life

None of that matters. If your chronic illness affects your ability to consistently complete daily activities, you could be entitled to PIP.

Key differences between PIP and other benefits

PIP stands apart from most other UK benefits in several important ways:

Financial independence:

- **Not means-tested.** Your income, savings, employment status or your partner's earnings do not affect your eligibility.
- **Tax-free.** You don't pay tax on PIP.
- **Compatible with other benefits.** You can receive PIP alongside other benefits or income sources.

Health and eligibility:

- **For chronic illness or disability.** PIP is for people whose condition affects their ability to function, not just those who are temporarily unwell.
- **Not based on diagnosis**. It's about how your condition affects your ability to carry out daily activities, not your diagnosis, medication or treatment.
- **You might not get both parts.** PIP has two sections – Daily Living and Mobility – and you may qualify for one, both or neither.

- **Possible deadline extensions.** It is sometimes possible to ask DWP for an extension on your deadline to submit your PIP form. The DWP are very understanding when asking for an extension for your Claim form but less so with Review forms.

Award structure:

- **Time-limited awards.** PIP is awarded for specific lengths of time (usually 3, 5 or 10 years).
- **Age eligibility.** You must be over 16 and under pension age to apply. If you are receiving PIP and reach pension age, you will move to a 10-year award.
- **Extensions possible.** In some Review cases, awards can be extended without a full reassessment.

PIP can also be considered a gateway award that **opens doors:**

- **Blue badge.** If you receive 8 points or above in the mobility section, you can get your blue badge.
- **Discounts and support.** PIP can open doors to things like London Transport discounts, occupational health visits, and access to other schemes and services.

Recognition and identity:

- **PIP can be used as evidence of the real-life impact of a disability.** This matters – for access, for advocacy and for being taken seriously.

Understanding PIP

Throughout this book, my goal is simple: to help make sure your claim does not SLIPP through the cracks. I am here to prep you, so the process does not SCAR you, then help you ROAR.

SLIPP, or what you need to get right:

- **Shaky** answers won't help you.
- **Lived** experience is important.
- It's about **Impact**, not illness.
- **Proof** is essential.
- **Points:** know how your score.

Remember SCAR? Are you Safe, Consistent And Reliable? That is how they will assess you, so to get your award, we are going to ROAR:

- Talk about your **Real-life struggles**
- Focus on the **Outcomes** you deserve

- Prepare for the **Assessment** with truth bombs
- Gather the **Right evidence**

Although we are all individuals with our own strengths and struggles, there are some things that we have in common. Most of us don't look sick. Our friends, families, partners, loved ones and even the doctors often don't understand what we are going through. When applying for PIP, we are suddenly expected to explain ourselves to a stranger!

Invisible illness is a blessing and a curse. People don't automatically discriminate when they see us. They don't generally feel sorry for us or don't judge us. At the same time, they don't see our pain, fatigue or trauma. Some think we are liars, drama queens or lazy. Too often, we have learnt to minimise how we feel, to bury and ignore how severely our lives have been impacted, but applying for PIP requires us to do the opposite: to stop masking and stop blocking out what's happened to our lives. We must face our reality and communicate it clearly. It's hard to do, and one of the reasons why many people fail to win their PIP claims.

PRO TIP

Only *you* can share the details of *your* life. Be as honest and transparent as you can throughout this application to convey your reality as accurately as you can.

The PIP scores

A large proportion of this book is concerned with helping you understand how PIP claims are assessed and how and why points are awarded. You may well be wondering why you need to know your PIP score before doing the form. The answer is simple: if *you* don't understand your PIP score, how can you expect a stranger to figure it out in just a few minutes? You cannot leave this to chance.

The process is not designed to help you. At some point, you are going to psychologically wobble, and that's normal. This guide is here to help you stay grounded, focused and prepared. We're going to plan for the worst and hope for the best as we're going through this process together.

If you are struggling, remember that you are not alone. This is not about intelligence or experience – it's genuinely really difficult and overwhelming. This guide will help you get through it in a more positive, strategic way. I'm by your side.

Myths and fears

Like so many things in life, the world of PIP is full of mistaken beliefs, myths and fears. The process is intimidating enough, without this confusion. Let's look at some of the most common myths and fears.

Firstly, let's talk about the elephant in the room: the proposed government changes to PIP / ADP. Yes, they will make changes in the future – they need to. When they do, I will update this book. Until then: it's business as usual. Do not let media fearmongering stop you from claiming the support you are entitled to now.

Claim form and paperwork beliefs:

- ☒ If I don't fill in every box perfectly, they'll bin my claim = Rubbish.
- ☒ If I write too little or repeat myself, they'll assume I don't need help or am lying = Rubbish.
- ☒ If my wording is off or my handwriting is messy, I'll ruin my claim = Use your own words but follow my advice; avoid vague terms like 'sometimes' and know your averages.
- ! If I write too much, they won't read it = Potentially, as humans only absorb a small amount of what they read.
- ! If I send extra pages, they'll ignore them = Potentially, if you send in loads of crap and irrelevant info.
- ☑ If my form gets lost in the post, it's my fault = True, send it recorded delivery.

Evidence and medical support myths:

- ☒ If my GP doesn't help, I can't win = False.
- ☒ If my consultant hasn't seen me in ages, I'll fail = False.
- ☒ If meds help, I'll be seen as fine = False.
- ☒ If I've 'only' got anxiety / depression, they won't take it seriously = False.
- ☒ If my family helps me, it doesn't count = False.
- ☒ If I'm managing with self-care, they'll think I'm fine = False.
- ! If I don't take meds, they might say I'm not ill enough = Potentially true, yes, as the need for treatment is an important indicator of severity.
- ☑ If I don't have a diagnosis yet, I can't claim = True.

The points system and entitlement myths:

- ☒ If I can do something once, I won't get points = False.
- ☒ If I can do it slowly with pain, I won't get points = False.
- ☒ If I do it with help, they'll count it as independent = False.

☒ If I use an aid, they'll assume that solves everything = False.

☒ If I don't use aids, they'll say I don't need help = False.

☒ If my condition fluctuates, I won't qualify = False.

! If I say 'good days' and 'bad days', they'll twist it = Potentially true, yes.

Eligibility myths:

☒ If I work, study or drive, I can't get PIP = False.

☒ If I go on holiday, I can't get PIP = False.

☒ If I've ever done sports, they'll use it against me = False.

☒ If I had kids, pets or live with family, I can't get PIP = False.

☒ If I live alone, I can't get PIP = False.

☑ If I use social media, I'll be caught out = Only if you are lying, in which case, yes, I hope you get caught.

Assessment day:

☒ If I smile, cry, don't cry or laugh, they'll think I'm fine or acting = False.

☒ If I get dropped off by car, I'll lose points = False.

☒ If I use public transport, I'll lose points = False.

- ☒ If I turn up on time, they'll assume I can plan a journey = False.
- ☒ If I miss the appointment, I'll be banned = False.
- ☒ If the assessor is friendly, they'll go easy on me = False.
- ☒ If I take someone with me, they'll think I'm weak = False.
- ☒ If I go alone, they'll think I don't need help = False.
- ☒ If I'm polite, they'll think I'm fine = False.
- ☒ If I forget something, I can't add it later = False.
- ! If I get angry, they'll mark me as aggressive = Potentially true. If you are struggling and need a break, just tell them. They are usually understanding.

After the assessment:

- ☒ If the assessor lies, I can't challenge it = False.
- ☒ If I ask for the report, it will harm my claim = False.
- ☒ If I win at appeal, they'll punish me later = False.
- ☒ If I get standard rate now, I will never get enhanced rate = False.
- ☒ If I get enhanced, they'll keep reviewing my case to cut me down = False.

- ☒ If I've been refused before, I'll always be refused = False.
- ☒ If I lose, I'll never get another chance = False.
- ☒ If I complain, it will harm my claim = False.
- ! If I appeal, they'll cut my award = Potentially, but I have never seen it happen.

Reviews and renewals:

- ☒ If my award ends, I'll definitely lose it = False.
- ☒ If I get a short award, it means they don't believe me = False.
- ☒ If I get a long award, they'll still review me early = False.
- ☒ If I don't improve or improve slightly, they'll take it away = False.
- ☒ If I update them, they'll stop my award = False.
- ☒ If I move house or go into hospital for a short stay, I'll lose my claim = False.

Money and other benefits:

- ☒ If I get PIP, I'll lose my other benefits = False.
- ☒ If I earn money, I'll lose PIP = False.
- ☒ If my partner works, I can't get PIP = False.
- ☒ If I get PIP, HMRC will tax me = False.

- ☒ If I get PIP, my credit rating will suffer = False.
- ! If I get PIP people will find out = Only if you tell them.

General fears:

- ! They'll spy on me at home = Possible.
- ! They'll spy on me on CCTV or follow me = Possible.
- ! They'll check my Facebook / Instagram / other social media = Possible.
- ! They'll ring my neighbours and ask questions = Unclear but unlikely.

Dangerous advice you should ignore:

- ☒ You should only talk about your worst days = Never do this. If your worst days mean you're stuck in bed or on the sofa, then every time you leave the house, you're technically being dishonest, even fraudulent. Be honest about your averages at all times.
- ☒ If you get PIP, you have to stay in the house or they will take it away from you = Rubbish.

Myths thrive where there is fear and confusion. This book is here to cut through some of the bullshit out there and help you claim what you're entitled to.

2
Understanding How PIP Works

We have begun the process of understanding what PIP is, and when you may get it, but what about if you do not look sick or your condition(s) vary? Many people worry that this will invalidate that claim. If you don't look sick and how you feel varies, then welcome to the club! Most people I work with fit into this category. It's totally normal and you are not alone. The assessors and case managers are used to this, and PIP is designed to take this into account.

Variable conditions and invisible illness

If you're thinking:

- But my conditions and life are complicated!

- They won't understand!
- I never know how I will be; it changes all the time.
- I don't have an average.

... STOP! You need to listen to me, otherwise you're going to screw up your PIP application, even if you are entitled to it. As humans, there are patterns to our lives. You will have averages; you just don't know them yet.

No one's life is too complicated for PIP. The process *does* work for everyone. I have worked with people with 1 condition and those with over 20; those on no medications to some taking so much medication that I can't even remember how many they were on.

Here is the proof that the DWP is fair when it comes to variable conditions: my own experience and the many successful PIP applications I have completed. I hear the misinformation out there that the DWP will not be fair; in my experience, based on my life and my clients' experiences, it *is* fair (in the end).

My mobility changes massively as the day goes on. Even what represents a 'day' changes. This is what my life is like: I am currently writing this at 5.14am. I think today my 'day' will end at about 10.30am as it started at about 2.00am. Sometimes it won't start until 11.30am, or I have bedridden days; sometimes my body shuts down and restarts in the afternoon or even at night. I have no real control over this.

Normally, when my body starts, I am able to do this:

I do not take my Zimmer frame! I just do this:

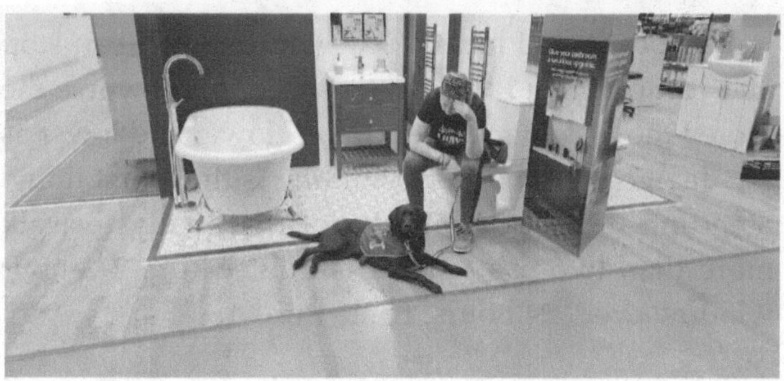

... Until I get the energy to walk back to my car after being out with the dogs. But after that walk, any other walking outside my home means I need to do this:

It is critical that I have a seat with me so I can stop and rest often and whenever I need. I feel worse the more I move, and my battery runs lower and lower as the day goes on. For me, standing is the worst thing. Standing in a queue? Fuck no! My ability to walk more than two bus lengths is limited to a 2–3-hour window every 24 hours. I hate this.

When I did my 'Change of Circumstances' review, the assessor asked me loads of questions about my changing mobility, as my mobility had improved. In the end, they treated me fairly at all times. This was true both before my YouTube channel and now, so I don't think it was just fear of bad publicity!

Have you noticed that, although my life is limited, I still work, drive a car and take my dogs out when my body lets me? Remember the 'Myths and fears' bit in the last chapter? The misinformation out there is bullshit! Loads of my clients work, drive, have children, pets and successful careers. Chronic illness does not discriminate, and PIP is designed to support all of us who are entitled to it.

How to simplify your life for PIP?

PIP is simple. Does your chronic illness impact your daily life? If yes, you could be eligible. We're going to go through your life in detail in Part Two of the book, but first, adjust your mindset and accept that this process *will* work for you; if you don't, you might as well stop reading the book now.

Start by deciding which condition totally controls, dictates and overrides your life. If you have loads of conditions, which are the *top three* conditions that control your life? These are the conditions we will focus on. This approach works every time, so get out your free workbook and start making notes *now*. You did download it in the Introduction, didn't you, because we are starting your PIP journey right now. Yep, now. Not got the workbook in front of you? Stop reading and download it now from https://charlies-journey.co.uk/free-stuff.

Now obviously, you can ignore everything I say. This is *your* life and *your* PIP journey, so you must be comfortable with the approach you take. Just because this is the way I do things does not mean it's the only way.

Got your workbook? Good! Let's start.

Helpful things to know about applying for PIP

We will go through this in detail in later chapters, but here are some initial pointers to get you started. These tips will save you time, money and potentially even your sanity:

- **There are no shortcuts when it comes to PIP.** This book is written to guide you through the PIP process. This process takes time, effort and emotional energy. This book is here to guide you, but you'll need to do the work. Prepare to invest in your future.
- **Keep copies of everything.** Never trust the DWP and the companies it subcontracts to. Keep copies of everything, and I mean everything – forms, letters, evidence, even receipts of evidence

sent via recorded delivery. If you can't prove it, it might as well not have existed.

- **Submit your evidence strategically.** One document equals one tab. Every individual document sent in to the DWP is saved separately on their system. That means that 20 letters equals 20 tabs. This is much too much, so that's why we'll create just one long evidence document so that your claim will just have two tabs: your form and your evidence document. This will make it easy for the assessor and case manager to review your case.
- **Don't waffle.** Part Three of this book will show you exactly what the PIP assessment is based on and what they are looking for. This means that you will understand what is relevant and what is not. People normally take in only a fraction of what they hear and even less of what they read, so really think about this. When I attend assessments with clients, the main thing I actually do for people (and this is said with love) is get them to stop talking. Stick to the relevant points. Be clear about your unique life and how your condition(s) affects it. Be blunt. Make sure it's relevant. Cut the crap.
- **Know your audience.** The assessor that you speak to is *not* the person who decides your outcome. They write a report and send it to a DWP case manager who will make the final decision. Don't waste time trying to 'win over'

the assessor; just give them the facts they need to make a really compelling case on your behalf.

- **Stay respectful at all times.** A lot of people feel angry when they see their outcome. Many will be disappointed with the initial result, and even those of us who get the outcome we hope for will probably still find aspects of the report that we disagree with or where we feel we have misunderstood or misrepresented. It is all too easy then to take your frustration out on the next person who deals with your claim, but remember, it's not that person's fault and nobody responds well when someone is arsey or threatens them. It will not help your case. Always speak and write with respect – it helps your case more than you think.
- **Update the DWP if you get better.** If you get better in the future, fantastic! All you have to do is update the DWP. It will be delighted to save some money and withdraw your funding. That's how the system works. You're not trapped.

Using AI

The way to win PIP is by using your own voice. Your words, your reality. Not what someone else says (although do follow my pointers!) and certainly not by using AI to speak for you. If you use AI, when you sound very different at the assessment, it will create doubts around the truth of what you have written. Consistency matters, and you are the expert on your own life.

How is PIP awarded?

In life, whenever we have some sort of important event coming up, whether it's our driving test, a job interview or an exam, we prepare. We study. We practise. Applying for PIP should not be any different.

Don't forget, PIP has two sections: Daily Living (10 activities) and Mobility (2 activities). Each activity has descriptors with a points score allocated, and the DWP needs to identify where you score.

The points

Stick with me on this. I understand that it can initially feel quite overwhelming, but I promise it's straightforward when you understand the basic process. Let's consider an example from Daily Living: the first question, preparing food. Imagine we're talking about someone who is autistic, who has a condition that affects their legs so they often need to sit down, and who needs supervision when preparing a meal.

To work out how many points a claimant deserves, the DWP produces a series of 'descriptors' for each activity. These describe the various levels of difficulty a person might have with completing that particular task. Here are the full descriptors for 'Preparing food'. As we read through them, it is clear that our case study should score with descriptors (b), (d) and (e):

Activity	Descriptors	Points
Preparing food	a. Can prepare and cook a simple meal unaided.	0
	b. Needs to use an aid or appliance to be able to either prepare or cook a simple meal.	**2**
	c. Cannot cook a simple meal using a conventional cooker but is able to do so using a microwave.	2
	d. Needs prompting to be able to either prepare or cook a simple meal.	**2**
	e. Needs supervision or assistance to either prepare or cook a simple meal.	**4**
	f. Cannot prepare and cook food.	8

When it comes to scoring, you don't add up all of the points within a single activity. Instead, you get the highest applicable score. In our example, this would be 4 points, for descriptor (e): 'Needs supervision or assistance to either prepare or cook a simple meal'. You do not add the points together for the whole activity. So it would *not* be 2 + 2 + 4 = 8.

Points: Key PIP terms

When it comes to PIP and your application, there are some key terms that will be used repeatedly. It is crucial that you understand what is meant by these.

Aids: An aid does not need to be a posh disability product. It can be anything that you already have that helps you. Even the radiator beside your toilet that you use to help you stand back up after you have been to the loo will count. Make sure you note it down.

Assistance: This is when someone is hands-on helping you complete the activity. They're not just watching or reminding you; they're physically involved. Examples include:

- Chopping vegetables for you
- Helping you get in and out of the bath

Prompting: This is a posh way of saying someone reminds, encourages or nags you to do something. For PIP purposes, prompting does not need to be face-to-face; a phone call, text or even a shout from another room counts. It also doesn't have to come from a specific person, like a carer or family member. What matters is that you need prompting to complete the activity. Frequency matters, so you'll need to explain how often you are prompted, on an average day.

For example: 'Monday AM, Mum calls me; at lunch, my sister visits; in the evening, my partner is home.' If all three were prompting you to prepare food, you would write: 'I get reminded to prepare a meal three times a day.'

Supervision: This means that you have someone physically present with you while you're doing an activity. It's not about them offering moral support or having a gossip; it's because without them there, you could be at risk. Examples of when this might be necessary include seizures, poor co-ordination, confusion etc.

Why your averages are critical to your claim

The PIP process is a headfuck, and I say that with love and lived experience. I cannot stress this enough: you must know and be able to explain confidently during your assessment how often you can complete the activities that the DWP actually cares about.

Here are some examples of the sort of explanation you must be able to give:

- 'On average, I can walk about five bus lengths, then I need to stop for a rest.'
- 'I shower about three times a week.'
- 'I have daily bowel (poo) accidents, and my partner has to help me clean up.'

If you don't already know your average, don't worry. That's normal, as we don't tend to track our lives in PIP-level detail. We are going to work it out together as we go through this book, and as you start using your diary and workbook, you'll begin to see patterns.

It is good to be aware that, as you figure this out, it might make you wobble. It is difficult seeing the reality of what your life has become, but I truly believe that knowing our baseline is the first step in moving forward in a positive, empowered manner.

How to use your free workbook

If you are serious about your PIP claim, you should already have your workbook in front of you; if not, please download it from https://charlies-journey.co.uk/free-stuff. You will need it to record your top conditions (up to three) and work out whether or not you should be eligible. If you don't have it yet, you are only making your life harder. I have included it because it's a tool I use when working with clients, and it helps secure the funding. If I need to use the workbook, you *really* need it!

The workbook layout matches what you see in this guide, so it's really simple to use. You will literally fill in the blanks or follow my instructions as we go. As we work through it, you will:

- Identify where you score in PIP

- Stay focused on relevant areas
- Make notes about how you manage activities
- Understand how your life links to PIP
- Gather the PIP Gold – the gritty personal details only you know, AKA the ugly truth
- Write your form / document
- Identify what evidence you need and how to get it
- Build a clear action plan

Everything will come together as we go. You've got this.

How do we get assessed?

I am sure you have gathered by now, but the assessment is *the most* important part of the whole process. Whether you win or lose your PIP claim often comes down to how well you prepare for the assessment. Practising matters. Watching the Practice Guides on YouTube (not just the Trickery Series) is essential.

There are two main types of PIP assessments:

- Phone calls
- Face-to-face appointment (home visits are available, if needed)

Phone assessments

This is my preference, and I strongly recommend requesting one if you genuinely need it.

Why a phone assessment can help:

- Less physical setup
- You're in your own space
- You can have your 'Charlie-approved' notes in front of you
- You can be as rested, focused and as clear-headed as possible

If you are well enough to attend in person, please do not ask for a phone assessment. Save that option for those people who really need it.

Face-to-face assessments

I do not agree with how these are conducted. They are a setup and you're being assessed from the moment you arrive. They watch:

- How far you walk
- Your ability to open doors
- How you sit in the chair

For example, if you can get up from the chair in the waiting room without leaning on anything or showing obvious difficulty, they might award you zero points in multiple areas of the form, even if you crash later. They don't care that most people (especially those of us with chronic illness) will push ourselves, even if it means we will suffer later. They will record only what they see in the moment, no matter how much you crash afterwards. They don't account for masking, delayed pain or more severe symptoms, even though their own procedures say they should.

We also have to work around appearance bias. In the UK, we tend to put more effort into our appearance when we are being assessed. Even people who rarely wash their hair (like me) will make sure their hair is clean before meeting a stranger who is about to assess them. A lot of women will put on makeup, as they want to try and look a bit 'better'. It's totally understandable, but here's the thing. If you can wear makeup, they could assume:

- Your hands are fine
- Your fine motor skills are excellent (doing delicate tasks with your fingers)
- Your mental health is good

From all of that, they could incorrectly determine that you're not that sick. From a PIP perspective, appearance can be weaponised against you. The whole thing is a setup. It's awful. It's dehumanising. It's why I'm writing this book, but don't worry. I'll walk you through exactly how to protect yourself during the assessment. You'll learn how to be honest, strategic and clear about your life and your needs.

Let me add a final word on integrity. Once, when I was attending a Tribunal, I spoke to the security team. They told me that they get sick of seeing people limp into the tribunal and then walk out absolutely fine, so let me be blunt: if you are reading this book because you want to blag the system, or if you're not disabled but you're trying to fake it, then it's because of dickheads like you that disabled people are treated like shit. This book is for people who are genuinely struggling. If that's not you, fuck off and get a job.

How long does the PIP claim process take?

The government doesn't like to give a clear answer to this question because it varies widely. Be warned: this is a marathon, not a sprint. If you're committed to sticking it out until you're treated fairly (including appeals), you could be looking at 12–18 months, or longer. You can call the DWP at any time and ask for an update. Just be prepared to spend 20–45 minutes on hold or talking to someone. Have your National Insurance number ready.

Here's an approximate timeline:

- **Step 1: Starting the claim.** After logging your claim, you should get the main form – 'How your disability affects you' – within about one month.
- **Step 2: Submitting the form.** After submission, it's usually about two months before your assessment.
- **Step 3: The assessment.** After the assessment, it takes up to a couple of months to get your outcome letter.
- **Appeal: Mandatory reconsideration.** Should be submitted within one month of your outcome letter. After submitting, it usually takes between two to four months to get a decision.
- **Appeal: Tribunal.** Ideally, you log this within one month of your Mandatory Reconsideration outcome. The DWP then has 30 days to review your case. They can either make you an offer or stand by their decision. If it goes to the tribunal team, it can take 6–18 months to complete.

Always submit your evidence with your form or appeal. If you don't, you risk them making a decision without seeing it, and that could cost you your award.

Transitioning from DLA to PIP

Let's be blunt. The way the government treats families when children move from Disabled Living Allowance (DLA) to PIP is utterly ridiculous. The idea that just because a child turns 16 years old means that they do not need support any more is just fucking wild. We *are* going to figure out the young person's claim, together. This book will guide you through the process and help you secure the funding they are entitled to. Please note that I have referred to 'your child' throughout this passage, but by this, I mean any young person, 16+, for whom you provide ongoing help and support.

I am going to show you some key differences that I think you need to know about:

Aids: DLA doesn't seem to care much about aids; PIP focuses on them – what aids your child uses and how often.

Behavioural/emotional support: DLA focuses on this; PIP doesn't really care. Sorry, that sounds so harsh. They don't care as much as DLA. Check Part Two and the condition-specific advice for each activity for guidance on how to handle this.

Care needs: DLA focuses on how much attention your child needs; PIP on how your child performs specific daily activities.

Nighttime needs: DLA considers the need for nighttime care as a major factor; PIP barely cares and nighttime support rarely scores points.

Safety: DLA accepts that constant supervision of your child is necessary (with evidence); PIP will *not* accept this as a good enough reason and only cares about safety within specific activities, not general supervision.

Seizures: DLA focuses on seizure risk; PIP doesn't score based on conditions or symptoms, but only on functional impact.

Let us consider one other key difference in some detail:

Going out. While DLA seems to accept, with evidence, that supervision is needed at all times when the child is out, PIP will try and downplay your child's needs to score fewer points

If your child can only go out somewhere alone because you have:

- Gone with them loads of times
- Followed them from a distance when they did it on their own
- Rescued them often
- Seen many occasions when they could not leave the house at all

Here is what I want you to do: over four weeks, work out their weekly average, to get a realistic picture of how many times they achieved this with *no* issues. Remember: PIP should look at a 12-month period, which is why it is important for you to have your averages worked out.

PRO TIP

Convert the average to weekly or monthly as it's easier for the assessors to understand.

To succeed with a PIP application for your child, we just need to change your mindset towards this funding:

- Forget nighttime.
- Focus on how often you encourage, prompt or even strategically nag your child to complete a task.
- Remember: PIP scores if someone cannot do something reliably over 50% of the time.
- Track how many burnout days your child has.
- Know their averages.

Ask yourself: *If I were not there, would my child do these activities (washing, dressing, eating etc)?*

Before submitting your application, it is crucial that you check your evidence, and do not submit what I call 'evidence with hope' – for example, 'With training, we hope that Ollie will be able to prepare his own meals...'. Hopeful phrasing like this can undermine your case. If this is your first time applying, and you have an Education, Health and Care Plan (EHCP) and/or neurodevelopmental report, you must submit them, but check them carefully for any 'hope' statements that imply future potential rather than current limitations. Be explicit: make sure you state clearly if your child cannot do the PIP activities. I have seen the DWP spot hopeful wording and use it against parents by noting that, for example, 'Medical professionals state that Ollie can do this task.'

It is heartbreaking having to frame the reality of your child's life through the lens of a PIP claim, but you need to do this to maintain essential funding. You're not exaggerating, you're documenting the truth and that can be upsetting to confront. I am hopeful that, in future, parents of non-verbal autistic young people won't be limited to three-year PIP awards. There is growing momentum for lifetime awards in cases like this, which I hope would make their lives easier and ease the burden of constant reassessment.

This book covers everything you need to help secure the funding your child is entitled to. It is also designed to support future reviews, so you don't have to slog through this guide – and the entire process – again!

What powers does the DWP have?

Let's not sugar-coat it: the DWP has power. Yes, they can investigate you and yes, I support this. Why? Because while most claimants are honest and exhausted, there's always a handful of people who will try to take the absolute piss. It's because of those few that the system has become the absolute beast that it is.

Can the DWP spy on us?

You've probably heard the stories: the bloke who turned up for their PIP assessment in high-vis construction gear, claimed they couldn't even prepare a basic meal, and then went straight back to the building site. The marathon runner claiming they couldn't manage daily tasks; they were literally running marathons while simultaneously receiving PIP *(WT actual F?)*. The gentleman supposedly so ill he could not get off the toilet without assistance yet somehow was playing football three times a week. These aren't just urban legends; they're the kind of hearsay that fuels suspicion and tightens the screws for everyone else. It is because of dickheads like this that the rest of us suffer more.

Do I support the checks? Yes. If they didn't exist, the system would be at real risk of even more abuse, but let's also be clear: fraud is rare. The actual rate of fraudulent PIP claims is **less than 1%.**[1] That's right, less than 1%, yet the rest of us are treated like suspects.

This section breaks down what powers the DWP really has, what they can (and can't) do and how to protect yourself by being honest, consistent and strategic. Remember that if you're telling the truth, you've got nothing to hide and everything to gain by being clear about your real, messy, day-to-day life.

Are they checking our bank accounts?

Yes, the DWP can access information about your bank account, but only under specific legal circumstances. There is no routine monitoring and the DWP does not have open or constant access to your accounts so they cannot log in or view your transactions. Under certain legal conditions, however – mainly if they suspect benefit fraud or need to verify financial details relevant to your claim – the DWP can request specific information from your bank, which they are legally required to provide. A lot of people are scared of this, but here's my thought: if you're being honest, what's the problem? What are they going to see?

- You order loads of takeaways?

1 DWP, 'Fraud and error in the benefit system, Financial Year Ending (FYE) 2025' (DWP, updated 12 June 2025), www.gov.uk/government/statistics/fraud-and-error-in-the-benefit-system-financial-year-2024-to-2025-estimates/fraud-and-error-in-the-benefit-system-financial-year-ending-fye-2025, accessed 8 October 2025

- Impulsive Amazon shopping because you're isolated and feel like shit?
- No card activity because you haven't left the house in four days?
- Transport costs?
- Our non-existent social lives showing no payments for lunch, cinema etc?

Let them look. If anything, it paints a clearer picture of the reality we live with.

When do they investigate?

From what I understand, they only investigate with cause, not randomly. Most often, it's triggered when someone reports you to the DWP. That can lead to:

- Scanning your social media and holiday photos
- Contacting your current/former employers
- Comparing your present/past forms and assessment reports
- Checking CCTV footage

This is why you must never listen to people that advise to 'only talk about your worst day'. This is terrible advice! As already mentioned, if you say you never leave the house, and then someone sees you at the corner shop on a 'better' day, it can be twisted into a fraud accusation. I cannot stress this enough: *do not* only talk about your worst days.

That's why I keep saying:

- Work out your averages.
- Be honest about your real, day-to-day life.
- Explain things in a way the DWP can actually understand and assess.

This isn't about exaggerating or downplaying; it's about truthfully describing the full picture, because your life isn't just one 'worst day' or a series of better ones. It's a mix, and that's what the DWP need to understand to provide a fair and accurate assessment – your averages.

PART TWO

THE PIP CLAIM FORM: A STEP-BY-STEP GUIDE

3
The Claim Form

Yes, the system is deliberately confusing. Yes, it's designed to wear you down, but here's the good news: starting your claim is surprisingly simple, and every day you delay could mean losing out on support you're entitled to.

In this central part of the book, we'll tackle the claim form together, question by question. I'll guide you through what to include, how to answer and just as importantly, what not to write. I won't tell you what to say – this is your reality – but I'll help you avoid the common mistakes that catch too many people out. Together, we're going to break it down, to one manageable bite at a time.

This chapter covers 'Section 1 – About your health condition or disability' and 'Section 2 – About your health professionals'. We will then move on to Section 3, covering each of the activities in turn, looking at both the activities of Daily Living and Mobility.

How to start a PIP claim

Starting your PIP claim is easy. There are several ways to do it, but I recommend calling them: 0800 917 2222, Monday to Friday, 8am to 5pm. The call will take about 20 minutes as they will complete the PIP1 form with you over phone and then you just wait for the main claim form ('How your disability affects you') to arrive. If you are deaf or struggle with the phone for other reasons, other methods are available; check the GOV.UK site for more information.

Alternatively, you can write to them at a freepost address to request a claim form: Freepost DWP PIP1. Although the website notes that 'You do not need a postcode or a stamp', I would advise against trusting their freepost as they have a history of 'losing' anything you send them. Send it recorded delivery.

You could choose to complete your claim online: www.gov.uk/pip/how-to-claim. However, online applications are being gradually introduced, so at the time of writing, this is not available to everyone. As the website notes, 'You can only apply for PIP online in some areas. You'll need to check your postcode when you start your application.' To start your claim online, you'll need your National Insurance number, email address and mobile phone number.

Don't forget, most of the time, your claim funding is backdated to when you first registered your claim, so let's get the process started today.

You will need the following information to begin your claim:

- Your contact details, for example, telephone number
- Your date of birth
- Your National Insurance number, if you have one (you can find this on letters about tax, pensions and benefits)
- Your bank or building society account number and sort code
- Your doctor or health worker's name, address and telephone number
- Dates and addresses for any time you've spent in a care home or hospital

- Dates for any time you spent abroad for more than four weeks at a time, and the countries you visited
- Information about any money or support you or a close family member (husband, wife, civil partner or dependent parent) get from an EEA country or Switzerland

After you have started your claim, you just need to sit back and wait for the main claim form to arrive. This should happen within about a month.

The 'How your disability affects you' form

Now the dreaded 'PIP: How your disability affects you' claim form has arrived, so make sure you've got it in front of you and let's work through it together. We'll start by getting the straightforward stuff out of the way. I won't include page numbers from the claim form as they change too often, but with your form in front of you, you'll be able to match this guide to the right sections. This *tiny* section of the book covers about sixteen pages of your claim form.

If you're applying for ADP in Scotland, your starting section is longer – about thirty pages – and, yes, clearly the Scottish Government really wants to make sure you count as Scottish before anything else.

Grab your PIP claim form now and let's get this done. Begin by entering your full name and your National Insurance (NI) number. Your case will be filed by your NI number. Done.

If someone is completing the form for you, they will also need to note their name and their relationship to you; for example: friend, mum, support worker. Done.

If someone is signing the form on your behalf, they must tick the reason why and give a brief explanation. Done.

Now you need to sign the form, print your full name and record today's date. Done!

Section 1: About your health condition of disability

This section is really important. What you write here will shape your assessment and affect how long it takes.

First, they want to know your *diagnosed* condition(s). If it's not diagnosed, they don't care. Harsh but true. Fill in:

- Name of condition
- Approximate start date (eg 'about 2020', '5+ yrs', 'Aug 2021')

Then record:

- Name of medication
- Dosage (eg 5 mg)
- Frequency (ie how often you take the medication, eg once a day)
- Side effects (eg feeling sick, fatigue) – although when I work with clients, I don't write anything under side effects, as we want PIP to focus on the activities

PRO TIP

Send an evidence document.

I *strongly* recommend creating a separate evidence document to send with your form. If you do this, you can simply write in both the condition and medications boxes, 'See evidence sent with this form.'

This proves your diagnoses and current medication, shows you're focused on relevant info, and forces the assessor to read your supporting document. Of course, you can still fill out the details on the form – ignore me if you prefer – but please don't list every condition you have ever had. Stick to what's current and relevant.

The next section is 'Treatment'. By this, they mean things like physiotherapy, dialysis, chemotherapy and other ongoing medical treatments. Don't worry if you do not have anything to write here, it's quite common. Simply write 'None'.

Section 2: About your health professionals

The final bit of this opening section is 'About your health professionals'. It asks for the names of professionals involved in your care; their roles (eg GP, consultant, therapist; and contact details, if available. It's simple. Start with your GP, then your specialist's details (if you have one), followed by any other specialists who might be involved in your care (if applicable).

Well done! That is all the easy bits completed.

Condition-specific guidance

We are now going to work through each of the activities in turn, considering what the DWP is looking for and how best to understand and apply the descriptors to your life. I am also going to provide some possible scorings for a variety of different types of conditions.

However, I need to lay down some important ground rules first:

- Everything I write in this book is just a suggestion, based on my experience and understanding. These suggested scorings are guidelines that might be relevant if you experience these conditions.

- Only *you* know *your life*: use your own words and your own examples. The examples provided here are simply meant to provoke thought, not be copied word for word.
- Just because I say to focus on a particular area, this does not mean you will necessarily be awarded those points. I repeat: these are guidelines only.

Please check every activity. This is particularly important if you think you have no problems with the activity – sometimes reading my explanation will change your mind. We need to unpick what has become your new norm, as you may have adapted in a manner that means you score within PIP without realising it. Your goal is to paint a clear, truthful picture of your real life. I am trying to help you focus on key areas and cut the crap.

This book would be about a million pages long if I tried to cover every single condition individually. It's just not practical, so instead, I'm going to group the conditions into four broad categories. Most people will fit into more than one – that's normal. Here's how I'm breaking down our conditions:

Group	Broad category	Examples
Group A	Physical conditions and pain-dominated conditions	Arthritis (RA, OA), Multiple Sclerosis (MS), Ehlers-Danlos Syndrome (EDS), fibromyalgia, chronic back pain, spinal injuries, sciatica, cerebral palsy, amputations, joint hypermobility, lupus, ankylosing spondylitis etc
Group B	Mental health conditions	Depression, generalised anxiety disorder (GAD), obsessive compulsive disorder (OCD), bipolar disorder, schizophrenia, eating disorders (eg anorexia, bulimia, ARFID), panic disorder, post-traumatic stress disorder (PTSD) and complex trauma (cPTSD), agoraphobia etc
Group C	Neurodivergence	Autism (including PDA profile), attention deficit hyperactivity disorder (ADHD), dyslexia, dyspraxia, dyscalculia, learning disabilities, global developmental delay, Tourette's syndrome, sensory processing difference etc

(Continued)

Group	Broad category	Examples
Group D	Fatigue-dominated conditions	Myalgic Encephalomyelitis (ME), Chronic Fatigue Syndrome (CFS), long COVID, post-viral fatigue, burnout, fibromyalgia (if fatigue is dominant), POTS, mitochondrial disorders etc

Many of us have more than one condition, and struggles in one area can often lead to struggles elsewhere. For example, many of us who have faced lifelong physical health problems develop mental health difficulties as a result of the ongoing struggles.

PRO TIP

Keep it simple, even if you have multiple conditions and health challenges. I want you to pick only two of the four categories listed above and focus your answers on these. Think of the two or max three conditions that totally control your life and concentrate on those.

For each group, I'm going to go through the PIP daily living and mobility activities. I will highlight which part of each activity is normally the most applicable for the type of symptoms you have. Remember that these are suggestions only: nobody can predict or guarantee how your particular PIP claim will be scored.

As you go through this part of the book, use your workbook and mark up the bits that are most relevant for you and your life. For example, consider the first activity, 'Preparing Food'. Here are the descriptors:

Activity	Descriptors	Points
Preparing food	a. Can prepare and cook a simple meal unaided.	0
	b. Needs to use an aid or appliance to be able to either prepare or cook a simple meal.	2
	c. Cannot cook a simple meal using a conventional cooker but is able to do so using a microwave.	2
	d. Needs prompting to be able to either prepare or cook a simple meal.	2
	e. Needs supervision or assistance to either prepare or cook a simple meal.	4
	f. Cannot prepare and cook food.	8

I have suggested the following possible scorings:

Group A (Physical conditions and pain-dominated conditions)	B, C or E if severe
Group B (Mental health conditions)	D (severe cases only) or E if at high risk of self-harm
Group C (Neurodivergence)	D or E if severe
Group D (Fatigue-dominated conditions)	B, C or rarely E

If you consider yourself to fall into Group A – physical health conditions – in your workbook, highlight either B, C or E (whichever you feel match your life). Do this for each activity, taking the time to read the examples and the notes and consider your answer. Simple!

Important note about PTSD and Complex PTSD (cPTSD): Please remember that the people assessing your PIP claim are *not* qualified to ask you about your past trauma. They are not therapists. They are not entitled to your story. You do not have to explain what happened to you; you don't even need to summarise it with phrases like, 'I was abused as a child.' It is none of their business, and I have never known them to ask what the past trauma was. All you need to explain is how your trauma affects your current daily life. That's it – I promise.

Your job is to protect your mental health. If this, or anything in the following chapters triggers you, pause and reach out to a medical professional or support service straight away.

How to win your claim

Do you remember what I said? Doing PIP properly is like trying to do a 10,000-piece jigsaw puzzle, except we do not have all of the pieces, and a load of the sky bits aren't even from your puzzle!

To solve this jigsaw, we need, first of all, to make sure we have all of the right pieces. That means understanding what your daily life is really like and linking it directly to PIP criteria. Then we have to dig for what I call the 'PIP Gold': that unique way *you* explain your life.

It's time to ROAR, not whisper, about the reality of your life. Let's break it down:

- Explain your **Real-life** struggles.
- Focus on the **Outcomes** you want. You're not 'just applying'. By the end of this book, you will know what you are entitled to, and you'll aim for it.
- Drop hard-hitting **Assessment** truth bombs. You are going to hit them with the facts of your life. No fluff and no shame. Just the ugly truth.
- Enclose the **Right** kind of evidence. Not just paperwork: proof that backs up your reality and your claims.

I will help you ROAR!

Applying for PIP is *hard* – that's why there is now a book on it! – but let's cover the critical things you *must* do to give yourself the best chance:

- Be entitled to PIP. Your chronic illness must impact your daily activities in specific, measurable ways before you will be entitled to this funding.

- Understand it's not 'just a form'. It's a headfuck. You aren't thick or losing your skill base; PIP is a nightmare and designed to put you off.
- Follow every step in this book. You cannot skip bits. Every section matters.
- Learn to explain how you feel – not just what you do, but how it affects you.
- Make your form unique to you. Save some of your PIP Gold for your assessment.
- Paint a picture of your life. Focus on explaining how you manage during the day (not night).
- Think SCAR, the lion: are you Safe, Consistent And Reliable.

Tips for getting it right:

- Focus on your current daily life, forget the past.
- Don't write about what you *could* do if you pushed yourself. Write about what you *actually* do.
- Be careful not to present rare good days as if they are happening all the time.
- Be brutally honest with yourself. Don't be surprised if you find yourself revisiting earlier answers as the truth sinks in. That's normal.

- If you are able, take time over completing the form. Do a little, then put it away for a few days. You'll probably find things occur to you that you want to include.
- Take time reading the descriptors. Even if you think it doesn't apply to you, I strongly encourage you to read through each section carefully in case something in what I've written prompts you.
- If your condition(s) is/are variable, work out your averages. Use your workbook to help with this.
- Use your own words – they are the right words. Don't rely on AI or generic templates.
- Don't listen to dickheads that don't know what they are talking about.
- Start collecting your evidence now, so that you can submit it all together.
- Use all of the free stuff I have provided.
- Sign up to my free newsletter so you feel less alone in this.

Your workbook is now your lifeline. Keep it with you as you go through the rest of this chapter. This is the core of your claim. As thoughts come to you, you need to be able to write them down straight away. Please trust me: the workbook is how I manage this process for clients.

We are about to do the hard bit: figuring out where you score and identifying your unique way of surviving with chronic illness. Remember: if it gets too much, you can just book time with me or a member of my team, or use my services for the Entitlement Assessment, with a written report showing the areas within PIP that you need to focus on. You can book an assessment by scanning the QR code below or visiting: https: / / calendly.com / charliesjourney.

Please do try to use this book and all the free stuff first. We know that thousands of people have succeeded with the YouTube channel, and now you have this book as well. *You can do this!*

Now we move into the real substance of the claim – how your conditions impact you. This is **Section 3** of the claim form, and it is assessed over 12 different activities: 10 are the activities of Daily Living, and the last two are about Mobility activities.

Please take time reading through this central part. Even if you think you have no problems with a particular activity, take a moment to read through my examples and think about what I have said in case it prompts something for you. So give the form the time and space it deserves.

Please note that I haven't numbered these questions as they sometimes change and I don't want to confuse you, but if we work through them together, you'll be fine. Remember that you shouldn't copy these examples word for word; it needs to be your words describing your reality.

As you move through the next few chapters, imagine me as the slightly annoying but well-meaning voice over your shoulder – the one who won't let you drift off course or sugar-coat your answers. When you're tempted to waffle, minimise or go off-script, I'll be there with a classic Charlie-style cut-the-crap check.

Let's get started. You've got this.

4
Daily Living Activities – Preparing And Eating Food

This chapter explores the first two 'daily living' activities assessed in PIP: preparing food and eating and drinking. Both are centred around nutrition, but they focus on very different aspects of it. One is about the ability to safely prepare a simple meal, while the other is about the physical act of consuming food and drink.

Preparing food

This activity is *only* about cooking a basic meal with one fresh ingredient. Eating is not relevant: loads of people confuse preparing food and taking nutrition (eating/drinking), but this is just about the actual process of making a simple meal for one. It includes things like peeling and chopping vegetables, and heating and cooking food.

PRO TIP

Forget the oven! They are not interested in anything to do with the oven. This is about preparing a simple meal using a microwave or on the hob.

Here are the descriptors used by the DWP:

Activity	Descriptors	Points
Preparing food	a. Can prepare and cook a simple meal unaided.	0
	b. Needs to use an aid or appliance to be able to either prepare or cook a simple meal.	2
	c. Cannot cook a simple meal using a conventional cooker but is able to do so using a microwave.	2
	d. Needs prompting to be able to either prepare or cook a simple meal.	2
	e. Needs supervision or assistance to either prepare or cook a simple meal.	4
	f. Cannot prepare and cook food.	8

Think you can do this activity with no issues so you will score zero? Hold up – read this first, please.

The DWP isn't asking whether you can make a spaghetti Bolognese or a curry from scratch. That's a myth. They are trying to figure out if you can safely, consistently and reliably (SCAR) prepare a basic meal, doing tasks like:

- Chopping broccoli
- Cooking it in boiling water
- Understand how long it needs to be cooked for and how to know if it is cooked
- Transferring it from pan to plate safely without hurting yourself or others

Most people screw this one up. Why? Because many of us don't prepare meals anymore because of our chronic illness. In this activity, the DWP is not interested in our current life (unlike the other activities), but in how we would manage on our own, in theory. If we're honest, the reality is that if you're reading this, you probably wouldn't starve to death. If you put down that you 'cannot cook and prepare food' at all (8 points) and it becomes clear that it's not accurate, it could really screw up your claim – especially if your medical records show that you could prepare a basic meal. People who do score 8 points tend to be those who have had a severe stroke or need full-time care.

When answering these questions, the DWP really focuses on:

- Use of aids or appliances
- Prompting or reminders
- Supervision or physical assistance
- Your safety and the safety of others

Let's be real. Everyone that cooks a basic meal, able-bodied or not, will burn themselves occasionally, drop things or even cut themselves. That's normal. So when it comes to safety, what they are also interested in is whether you are a danger to yourself or others. What the DWP cares about is frequency and risk. If you're regularly burning yourself or dropping things, leaving the gas on or starting fires, that is what matters.

The assessor is looking to understand:

- How often you really prepare a basic meal
- What would happen if you had to prepare a meal alone
- If you are not safe, what's actually happened and how often (do *not* answer this on your form: let them ask you about this during the assessment)

This section breaks down three key ways you might score points for the 'Preparing Food' activity. I'm not listing these in descriptor order, and yes, there's a reason for that. We're focusing on what actually applies to your life.

Also consider:

- How many meals have you actually prepared in the last week?
- How did you feel before, during and after preparing food?
- How long did it take you to prepare the basic meal? (eg twice as long as someone able-bodied etc)

Prompting

Preparing food	d.	Needs prompting to be able to either prepare or cook a simple meal.	2

Do you need to be reminded, encouraged, prompted or nagged to prepare food? If yes, how often does this happen and why?

Reality check: Just be aware that prompting points are usually awarded for mental health or cognitive conditions only, not physical ones. This means that if you need prompting because of fatigue, pain or physical limitations, that won't count here. Be honest about your life, but plan for zero points.

Preparing food	e. Needs supervision or assistance to either prepare or cook a simple meal.	4

Do you need someone to stay with you while you cook to keep you safe? If yes, why do you need supervision and how often does this happen?

How about assistance? For example, do you have hand issues (weakness, tremors or co-ordination issues) so you team up with someone in the kitchen and they chop things while you do other tasks? Is physical assistance from someone else a regular part of how you manage cooking? Note that to get the 4 points here, your condition needs to be very severe.

Aids and appliances

Preparing food	b. Needs to use an aid or appliance to be able to either prepare or cook a simple meal.	2

Do you use aids or appliances when preparing a basic meal? If yes, what aids do you use (eg perching stool, seat, jar-opener)? How often do you use them? Why do you need to use them?

Examples of possible aids: Any kind of perching stool or chair, kitchen trolley to move items safely without lifting, timer or alarm, kettle-tipper or non-touch kettle, knives with special grips, large-handled utensils, jar openers.

Here is an example of what I use in my daily life:

A seat, a trolley, a non-touch kettle and special grip utensils

Microwave

Preparing food	c. Cannot cook a simple meal using a conventional cooker but is able to do so using a microwave.	2

This descriptor is about function, not preference. If you now rely on a microwave or eat cold food / finger food because of your condition, you might score here.

Ask yourself:

- Do you *only* use a microwave to heat food or eat cold food?

- If yes, why? (Pain, fatigue, safety concerns)
- How often do you prepare meals this way?

If you're using a microwave because it's easier or quicker, that's not enough, but if it's the only way you can safely, consistently and reliably manage to have a hot meal, that's relevant.

Real-life examples

Physical/pain conditions (Group A) and severe fatigue (Group D) example: 'My mum prepares all meals for me. I use a perch chair given to me by Occupational Therapy. I do have chopping and opening aids, but I don't really use them because I decline badly as the day goes on and can't even get to the kitchen. I always drop things and misjudge distances.'

That is *my* life, with physical health conditions, pain and severe fatigue, and I score only 2 points here.

Evidence suggestions: Photos of any aids or appliances that you use.

> Channel your inner Chandler Bing from *Friends*: Could you *be* any more blunt?

Common mistakes

- Talking about eating instead of food preparation.
- Claiming 8 points when it's not justified.
- Mentioning the oven (not relevant here).
- Talking about preferences instead of necessities.
- Writing too much: you do *not* need to write more than the space allows. If you're tempted to add an extra page – STOP! Go back to START. Do not collect £200.

Possible scorings

Group A (Physical conditions and pain-dominated conditions)	B, C or E if severe
Group B (Mental health conditions)	D (severe cases only) or E if at high risk of self-harm
Group C (Neurodivergence)	D or E if severe
Group D (Fatigue-dominated conditions)	B, C or rarely E

Summary

- This is *only* about making a basic meal, not eating and not gourmet cooking.
- You score points if you need aids, prompting, supervision, or can't do it safely and/or reliably.

- Very few people get 8 points so don't claim it unless it's brutally true.
- Safety means real, repeated risk, not the odd cut or burn.

Eating and drinking

This activity is *only* about being able to chew, swallow and drink fluids. Cooking is not relevant. Don't get sidetracked.

The assessor wants to understand exactly how you manage to eat; not what you eat, not how you prepare it, but whether you can physically consume food and drink safely and reliably to decide if you score in this category. If you don't make your struggles crystal clear, they will very quickly move on.

Here are the DWP descriptors:

Activity	Descriptors	Points
Taking nutrition	a. Can take nutrition unaided.	0
	b. Needs – i. to use an aid or appliance to be able to take nutrition; or ii. supervision to be able to take nutrition; or iii. assistance to be able to cut up food.	2

Activity	Descriptors	Points
	c. Needs a therapeutic source to be able to take nutrition.	2
	d. Needs prompting to be able to take nutrition.	4
	e. Needs assistance to be able to manage a therapeutic source to take nutrition.	6
	f. Cannot convey food and drink to their mouth and needs another person to do so.	10

Think you score zero points for this activity? No issues at all? Pause, and just take a moment to flick through here to check. If you are filling this out for someone else and they clearly need help, explain that and skip ahead.

Here's what the assessor is really looking for:

- Can you breathe properly while eating and drinking?
- Can you eat and drink without choking?
- Do you consume a normal healthy amount (especially if you have an eating disorder and/or are medically under/overweight)?
- Is your condition so severe that you need help to safely do this activity?

- Do you use aids or appliances (eg adapted cutlery, non-slip mat)?
- Do you normally need prompting to eat and drink?
- Do you need supervision or assistance, like someone cutting food for you or staying nearby in case you choke?

If any of these apply, you might score points here.

Let's start with some nice quick descriptors that have no grey areas:

Taking nutrition	c.	Needs a therapeutic source to be able to take nutrition.	2
	e.	Needs assistance to be able to manage a therapeutic source to take nutrition.	6

This question is straightforward: do you use a feeding tube (c)? This is what they mean by a 'therapeutic source'. If yes, does someone help you with this (e)?

Done! It does get more complicated, but if we take it step by step, we'll be fine. Don't forget, there is a reason for me not doing the points in the order on the table.

Prompting

Taking nutrition	d.	Needs prompting to be able to take nutrition.	4

Warning: This activity is *not* like the other 11 activities within PIP when it comes to prompting. The bar is much higher here, and most people won't score unless their situation is very specific.

To qualify for 4 points, you usually need one of the following:

- Cognitive impairment (eg dementia or learning disability)
- Severe depression (typically with regular involvement from the mental health team)
- Eating disorder (such as anorexia nervosa, where you are medically deemed as underweight and at risk)

Even many of my non-verbal clients who will not eat unless food is placed in front of them don't score here. That's how tight they are about the criteria.

Still, if you do need prompting to eat, be honest about your situation. You may not score, but it's important to paint a picture of your life. Describe who prompts you, how often and what happens if they don't?

This isn't about occasional reminders or gentle encouragement. It's about essential, repeated prompting due to a mental health or cognitive condition that makes eating unsafe or unreliable without it.

Aids and appliances

Taking nutrition	b. Needs – i. **to use an aid or appliance to be able to take nutrition; or** ii. supervision to be able to take nutrition; or iii. assistance to be able to cut up food.	2

Here is what I use:

Do you use aids to help you, like chunky cutlery, no-spill cups? If yes, what aids do you use? How often do you use them and why?

Examples of possible aids: Chunky cutlery or utensils, beaker or cup with handles, plate with raised edge, feeding tube.

Supervision and assistance

Taking nutrition	b. Needs – i. to use an aid or appliance to be able to take nutrition; or **ii. supervision to be able to take nutrition; or** **iii. assistance to be able to cut up food.**	2

Supervision (b. ii): This applies to people who need to have someone stand with them while they are eating to ensure they are safe. This could be, for example, because they are at risk of choking, history of self-harm or will avoid eating.

Assistance (b. iii): This applies if someone cuts up your food for you or prepares meals that are 'scoopable' or finger food as you cannot safely or consistently cut your own food due to your condition. You could score here.

Think about your eating experience (not just the food, but the process):

- What is it like using a knife and fork every day? Does it cause pain, fatigue, frustration or make meals feel like a chore?

- Do you sometimes leave meals unfinished because of your symptoms – pain, nausea, breathlessness, tremors etc?
- Are there times when you skip eating altogether because you simply don't have the energy or the motivation to eat, or you're too exhausted or overwhelmed?
- Does cutting up food (especially something like chicken – the DWP *loves* a chicken example…) increase your pain or trigger symptoms?
- How do you feel after you've eaten, physically and emotionally? (Drained, in pain?)
- How many proper meals have you eaten in the last week? (Snacks like biscuits and crisps do not count.)
- How long does it take you to eat a basic meal? Is it significantly longer than someone able-bodied or without your condition?
- How long does it take you to recover after eating a meal? Perhaps to lie down, take medication or manage symptoms?
- What kind of meals are you living on now compared to before you became unwell? (eg microwave meals vs home-cooked; toast vs balanced meals)

These prompts aren't for copy-pasting into your form. They're here to help you reflect so you can pick out the bits that genuinely relate to your situation.

> Think of the answer like your Patronus: no two are the same; each is unique, personal and shaped by your lived experience.

Real-life examples

Neurodivergence (Group C) example: 'My son does not feel hunger and won't remember to eat. I must put the food in front of him, in bite-sized pieces, then encourage him to eat it. If I didn't do this, he simply wouldn't eat.'

Evidence suggestions:

- Photos of any aids that you use
- Medical letters that state facts about how your condition(s) impact on your ability to eat and drink

> You don't need to use more space on the form. Wakanda may be forever, but your answer should not be.

Common mistakes

- Focusing on food preparation. This section is not about cooking. It's about the physical act of eating and drinking.

- Not understanding that the DWP hate to give points for prompting here.
- Misunderstanding the 'cutting food' part because you've changed what you eat because of how your chronic illness affects your life, so you don't need to use a knife or fork anymore.
- Thinking 'I do eat, so I must not qualify'. This is the most common misconception. The question isn't whether you eat, but how you eat and whether you need help to do so.

Possible scorings

Group A (Physical conditions and pain-dominated conditions)	B
Group B (Mental health conditions)	Potentially B (for eating disorders) or rarely D
Group C (Neurodivergence)	B, D or E if severe
Group D (Fatigue-dominated conditions)	B

Summary

- This activity is only about the act of chewing, swallowing and drinking, not shopping, preparing or cooking.

- You may score points if you need:
  - Aids
  - Help cutting food
  - Supervision
  - Prompting
  - Help eating
  - A feeding tube
- Prompting points are rarely awarded.
- Don't skip this section just because you 'do eat' – if you need help, take longer or experience pain, fatigue or risk, it may count.

5

Daily Living Activities – Managing Therapy Or Monitoring A Health Condition

Let's be honest – this one's a bit of a beast! Although I am working through each of these activities in the order that they appear in the form, I am actually going to suggest that you do this one last. Move on to the next chapter and then return to this later. This is the hardest one to figure out, and by the time you have tackled the other activities, you will be in a much better position to answer it clearly.

I'm going to say: skip ahead, do the rest and then come back here when you're ready. Get yourself a cup of tea. You'll need it!

Managing your treatments

According to the DWP, this question assesses 'your ability to monitor any health conditions, manage medication and manage treatments',[2] but what does this actually mean?

- It's *not* about dressing, washing or toileting (those are covered elsewhere).
- It *is* about how much time someone spends helping you with:
  - Taking prescribed medication
  - Monitoring your symptoms
  - Managing therapies or treatments

The DWP wants to know how many hours per week someone helps you with these tasks and why. They are looking for whether you can do these things safely, consistently and reliably (SCAR). That includes:

- Taking your prescribed medication (tablets, injections, inhalers, creams etc) without missing doses or taking too many

2 DWP, 'Personal Independence Payment: How your disability affects you' (DWP, January 2021), https://assets.publishing.service.gov.uk/media/6602af72f1d3a09b1f32ac81/pip2-form-and-information-booklet__1_.pdf, accessed 20 October 2025

- How long someone spends with you to keep you safe by monitoring your symptoms (especially if you have a registered carer)
- Receiving help with therapy or treatment routines

The DWP is *not* interested in:

- Holistic or alternative medication or treatments (eg box breathing, acupuncture)
- Vitamins or supplements, unless prescribed by a registered doctor or nurse practitioner
- Over-the-counter items you buy at the pharmacy

Therapies that do count include:

- Physiotherapy, if you need assistance from another person to do it
- Home dialysis
- Special diets, but only if the timing of the food is medically critical

Here are the descriptors used by the DWP:

Activity	Descriptors	Points
Managing therapy or monitoring a health condition	a. Either – i. does not receive medication or therapy or need to monitor a health condition; or ii. can manage medication or therapy or monitor a health condition unaided.	0
	b. Needs either – i. to use an aid or appliance to be able to manage medication; or ii. supervision, prompting or assistance to be able to manage medication or monitor a health condition.	1
	c. Needs supervision, prompting or assistance to be able to manage therapy that takes no more than 3.5 hours a week.	2
	d. Needs supervision, prompting or assistance to be able to manage therapy that takes more than 3.5 but no more than 7 hours a week.	4
	e. Needs supervision, prompting or assistance to be able to manage therapy that takes more than 7 but no more than 14 hours a week.	6
	f. Needs supervision, prompting or assistance to be able to manage therapy that takes more than 14 hours a week.	8

Because this activity is such a nightmare, let's check the government's own PIP assessment criteria, as there are a few things I need you to understand:

> 'For the purpose of descriptor 3C to F, the "majority of days" test does not require the individual to actually be receiving therapy on the majority of days in a year. However, the descriptor would still need to accurately describe the claimant's circumstances on the majority of weeks in the required period. For example, if a claimant needs assistance for 3 hours to undergo home dialysis on Monday and Friday every week, they would not actually be receiving the therapy on the majority of days in year. However, the statement that they need "assistance to be able to manage therapy that takes more than 3.5 hours but no more than 7 hours a week" would still apply, as it accurately describes the level of support needed on the majority of the weeks in the required period.'[3]

To summarise that paragraph, for this activity, you would add the hours in the week together:

- Monday: 3 hours of dialysis
- Friday: 3 hours of dialysis

---

3 DWP, 'PIP assessment guide part 2' (DWP, 25 November 2024), www.gov.uk/government/publications/personal-independence-payment-assessment-guide-for-assessment-providers/pip-assessment-guide-part-2-the-assessment-criteria, accessed 4 March 2026

- Total per week: 6 hours of treatment time

This means that, while the claimant is not receiving treatment on the 'majority of days' (just two: Monday and Friday), they *would* still score in descriptor (d) as this reflects the circumstances on the 'majority of weeks in the required period':

Managing therapy or monitoring a health condition	d. Needs supervision, prompting or assistance to be able to manage therapy that takes more than 3.5 but no more than 7 hours a week.	4

Does that make sense?

PRO TIP

Don't be tempted to combine the time spent on unrelated activities (eg washing or dressing). This is only about the time spent managing treatments and therapies.

We also need to consider what is meant by **'monitoring a health condition'**:

> 'Monitoring a health condition means the ability to recognise significant adverse changes in the claimant's health condition and take corrective action to implement treatment plans or modifications, as advised by a health professional. The [Health Professional] should expect to see evidence demonstrating

> recognition of the role the person is playing in actively monitoring the claimant's health condition, for example a diabetic claimant whose blood sugar levels change and where the third party would be able to take action as a result, without which the claimant's short or long-term health would be at risk.'[4]

In my opinion, this paragraph is what screws up so many claims, not because the need isn't real, but because it's hard to prove. Think about these examples:

- A mum notices her autistic child is getting overwhelmed. She recognises the warning signs and intervenes to prevent a meltdown.
- A partner sees their loved one with severe depression spiralling and distracts or redirects them to keep them safe.

These are 100% real, daily and critical interventions, but how the fuck do they prove it? Yes, there will be some severe cases where the Mental Health Teams are involved, so it can be evidenced, but for the vast majority of people who should score here, it's hard to prove.

Reminder: Even if you think you score zero here, triple-check everything before going to the next activity. Many people do qualify but don't realise it.

---

4 DWP, 'PIP assessment guide part 2'

Aids and appliances

Descriptor (b) considers the need to use an aid or appliance:

Managing therapy or monitoring a health condition	b. Needs either – i. **to use an aid or appliance to be able to manage medication; or** ii. supervision, prompting or assistance to be able to manage medication or monitor a health condition.	1

Ask yourself, do you use a pill box (dosette), alarms, apps, pill cutter, pill popper or even a spreadsheet to help you remember to take your medication *yourself*? If yes, you might score a point here. Explain on your form what would happen if you did not use these aids; would you forget? Miss doses? Take too many?

If no, you don't use anything or anyone to remember to help you remember to take your medication, you likely don't score under part (i).

Examples of possible aids: Pill pot/dosette box; pill popper or cutter; easy-grip bottle openers; liquid medicine dispensers; timer, alarm, app or spreadsheet.

Here is what I use:

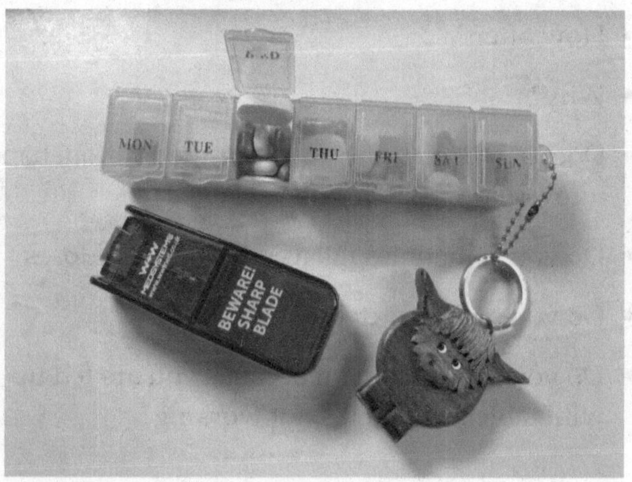

Supervision, prompting and assistance

Part (ii) of descriptor (b) considers 'supervision, prompting or assistance'.

First, ask yourself if you need to be reminded, encouraged, prompted or nagged to take your medication? If no, cross out the word '**prompting**' in your workbook (don't cross out all of (b. ii) – we're not done yet):

Managing therapy or monitoring a health condition	b. Needs either – i. to use an aid or appliance to be able to manage medication; or ii. supervision, ~~prompting~~ or assistance to be able to manage medication or monitor a health condition	1

If yes, you *do* get prompted, now explain:

- How often?
- Why?
- Does someone bring you your medication, hand it to you or put it beside you?
- Do you sometimes fall asleep and miss doses?
- Do you get distracted and forget?
- Do you avoid taking it because you are fed up with tablets or feel it's not working?

Let us now consider '**supervision**' and '**assistance**':

Managing therapy or monitoring a health condition	b. Needs either – i. to use an aid or appliance to be able to manage medication; or ii. **supervision**, prompting **or assistance to be able to manage medication or monitor a health condition.**	1

Do you need to be **supervised** when taking your medication or receiving therapy? This could be for a wide variety of reasons, such as because you forget and then overdose, you hear voices telling you not to take your meds, or perhaps because you had a stroke and someone needs to check you are safe swallowing. This could also be because you might not be aware that your condition has deteriorated and that you require rescue medication, such as with epilepsy or diabetes. If yes, explain clearly what supervision looks like, why it's needed and how often. If no, cross out 'supervision' in your workbook.

Finally, let us consider **assistance** (b. ii). Do you need hands-on help with your medication or therapy? Examples of this include:

- Help popping tablets out of the packets
- Help setting up your pill box (especially if you take lots of meds)
- Someone monitoring your health condition (eg checking symptoms, blood sugar, mood changes)

If yes, explain what kind of help you need and why. If no, cross out 'assistance' in your workbook.

Can you see why this descriptor is so hard? Some people might need all three: an aid (pill box), prompting (reminders), and supervision or assistance (help taking or organising their tablets). That's valid, so if that's you, say so. The DWP needs to understand the full picture.

The rest of the descriptors *only* vary based on the time you have help each week:

- (c): 3.5 hours a week or less
- (d): 3.5–7 hours a week

- (e): 7–14 hours a week
- (f): More than 14 hours a week

Let's look first at descriptor (f), as it might save a lot of you some time. Do you have a registered carer? This could be anyone who has formally identified themselves as a carer with the relevant services, such as their GP, local council or care services. If yes, you meet descriptor (f). Done! You can leave this chapter.

Now we are left with descriptors (c), (d) and (e). They are differentiated only by how much time is needed each week to prompt, support or assist you in managing your therapies and monitoring your health condition. There is no easy way to do this, based on what you have learnt. Only *you* (and the people that support you) can work out how much time is spent supporting you that PIP counts as relevant. If you need to, use the free diary in your workbook to figure it out. Sorry it's so hard.

Real-life examples

Physical conditions (Group A) example: 'Because of my cerebral palsy, I have to have help from my dad to do my physio. I hate doing it as it hurts. He normally has to psych me up for about 20 minutes to get me to do it, and then he has to help me as my right side is weak. The physio itself then takes us 30 minutes a day.'

Mental health conditions (Group B) example: 'My wife has to give me my tablets three times a day and she has to spend a few minutes each time trying to get me to swallow them i.n front of her. I know I need my tablets, but I hate taking them. Some days she just has to leave me alone as I get so angry. On those days, often I do not even bother taking the tablets.'

Mixed conditions example: This example answer is based on a mix of both physical and mental health conditions.

Content warning: Mental health and suicidal thoughts. Please take care while reading. If this resonates with you, consider reaching out for professional support: 'I think about ending it all the time. My mum checks on me throughout the day to make sure I am safe and not getting really bad. We worked it out and she spends 5–10 minutes a day bringing me my medication and getting me to take it as often I can't be bothered, or I'm asleep and I don't want to be woken up. She also has to make me eat or my blood sugar levels drop, which can be really dangerous, so when she checks on me, she is also making sure I am still alive. The time spent getting me to eat varies: on a better day, it might take 2 minutes, but on bad days, she might have to sit with me for 20 minutes.'

Evidence suggestions:

- A letter from your registered carer and a copy of their letter proving they are in receipt of Carer's Allowance, if this is the case
- Letters from specialists confirming your treatment needs and support
- Photos of any aids that you use – for example, a photo of your pill pot with one medication box in the photo showing your name and address

(I am seeing a pattern where the DWP do not seem to want to award the 1 point for using a pill pot, unless somebody is diagnosed with a mental health condition. Please be aware of this.)

> When you complete your form, think like Ross from *Friends* moving that sofa: PIVOT to the point!

Common mistakes

- Describing support that isn't relevant under this activity (eg help with dressing or emotional support that isn't about monitoring or managing a health condition).
- Not backing up what you are stating with evidence.
- Wasting time on this descriptor when, in reality, it's unlikely to score. They don't even like giving out the 1 point score, FFS!

If you still think you need more space to write about your life, I have failed.

Possible scorings

Group A (Physical conditions and pain-dominated conditions)	B
Group B (Mental health conditions)	B as a start; C, D, E, F if you need daily face-to-face checking, are actively suicidal or need supervision; Note: If you have daily or weekly checks from the mental health team, you're likely to score in D/E/F.
Group C (Neurodivergence)	B for ADHD (higher if supervision is needed); For people with severe ASD: carefully figure out the average hours a day/week spent supervising the person, focusing on safety.
Group D (Fatigue-dominated conditions)	B

Summary

- Do this activity last. It's the hardest to get right and you'll answer it better once you've worked through the rest of the Daily Living activities.

- The assessor is looking for specific, personal detail about what help you need, how often you need it, how long it takes and why you can't do it safely, reliably and consistently (SCAR) on your own.
- Only include prescribed medications and therapies where you need aids, prompting, supervision or hands-on help.
- Scoring is based on the time per week someone else spends helping you to 'manage therapy or monitor a health condition' (nothing else).
- Holistic treatments, vitamins or shop-bought/ homemade remedies don't count unless prescribed by a registered doctor or nurse practitioner

If you have made it this far and left this activity to last, as I recommended, then... congratulations! Daily Living is done! 10 points to Gryffindor! (Or whichever house you're in – we're inclusive here!)

6

Daily Living Activities – Washing, Toileting And Dressing

This chapter looks at three key areas of daily living that the PIP assessment covers – washing and bathing, using the toilet, and getting dressed and undressed. These are everyday tasks that most people do without thinking, but for many of us, they take extra time, effort or assistance. Here we'll explore what each activity means in PIP terms, what types of help are recognised, and how to describe you needs clearly and honestly on your form.

Washing and bathing

This activity is about how you manage personal hygiene, specifically, how you have a wash, bathe and/or shower. Even if you do not wash or bathe regularly due to your condition, you will need to explain how you manage to keep yourself clean and explain why you might wash less frequently than you'd like or even avoid it altogether.

For 'Washing and bathing', these are the official descriptors and point scores:

Activity	Descriptors	Points
Washing and bathing	a. Can wash and bathe unaided.	0
	b. Needs to use an aid or appliance to be able to wash or bathe.	2
	c. Needs supervision or prompting to be able to wash or bathe.	2
	d. Needs assistance to be able to wash either their hair or body below the waist.	2
	e. Needs assistance to be able to get in or out of a bath or shower.	3
	f. Needs assistance to be able to wash their body between the shoulders and waist.	4
	g. Cannot wash and bathe at all and needs another person to wash their entire body.	8

If you think you can do this activity with no issues, pause for a moment before skipping ahead. Check this chapter, just in case. If you are completing this form for someone who clearly scores 8 points, explain why they cannot do this activity – for example, if they cannot wash their body due to severe stroke and left-side paralysis – and then feel free to move on.

What PIP wants to figure out is if you can safely, consistently and reliably (SCAR) wash and bathe yourself. That means:

- Can you get in and out of a bath or shower safely?
- Can you clean the essential areas – underarms, groin, hair? (Don't obsess about your feet unless your condition makes it an issue. Most able-bodied people don't scrub their feet every time either!)

Now, let's pause for a reality check. Bathrooms are genuinely dangerous places for many of us living with a chronic illness. If we are going to have a bad fall, one that might cause severe and lasting damage, it is most likely going to happen in the bathroom.[5] We are high risk. A fall in the bathroom could mean losing abilities we've fought hard to maintain, and yet we're often expected to push through, even when we're unwell, exhausted or overwhelmed. That expectation is not just unfair – it's dangerous. Don't be forced into

5 Falls Prevention Foundation, 'Prevent Elderly Falls in Bathroom: A Complete Safety Guide for Seniors and Caregivers' (Falls Prevention Foundation, 25 June 2025), https://fallpreventionfoundation.org/2025/06/25/prevent-elderly-falls-in-bathroom-a-complete-safety-guide-for-seniors-and-caregivers, accessed 12 October 2025

doing this when you don't feel well enough; you have enough going on without making it worse due to a damn fall!

I used to be a humanitarian worker in Africa, where water is more precious than gold. Some of my friends there never bathe or shower and yet they smell lovely. Daily bathing is a cultural habit, not a medical necessity, so let's challenge the guilt. You can stay safe and clean with a simple wash. You don't need to risk your health to meet someone else's hygiene standard. This isn't about laziness. It's about survival, dignity and reclaiming control. I wrote this because it might just change how you approach daily life and how you advocate for your needs, not just in your PIP claim but in your wider world.

The DWP focuses on whether you need aids or prompting, supervision or assistance, and whether you can manage essential areas of your body safely, consistently and reliably. That's the lens they use, and so it is the one you should use too. As we work through these questions, remember to be honest and specific, but most of all, to be kind to yourself.

Prompting

Washing and bathing	c. Needs supervision or **prompting** to be able to wash or bathe.	2

Do you need to be reminded, encouraged, prompted or nagged to wash, shower or bathe? If yes, how often? Why?

Supervision and assistance

Washing and bathing	c. Needs **supervision** or prompting to be able to wash or bathe.	2

Let's clear something up: this doesn't mean that someone must be physically in the bathroom with you to qualify for support in this activity. If they are – helping, supervising or just standing by – of course, explain this on your form, but even if they're just in the house, with the door open, ajar or unlocked so they can respond quickly if something goes wrong, that still counts.

In my experience, people who tend to score points here are those who:

- Have had a bad fall or feel wobbly or unsteady on their feet
- Are at risk of seizures, joints locking or sudden leg weakness – the kind where your legs just decide to stop working etc

Teamwork is always important in PIP. If you've adapted your routine to reduce risk, that's relevant. If you've had to change how you wash because your body no longer plays fair – that's what this section is for.

Now, let's talk about describing your body in PIP talk. I want you to split your body into sections, as per the PIP descriptors:

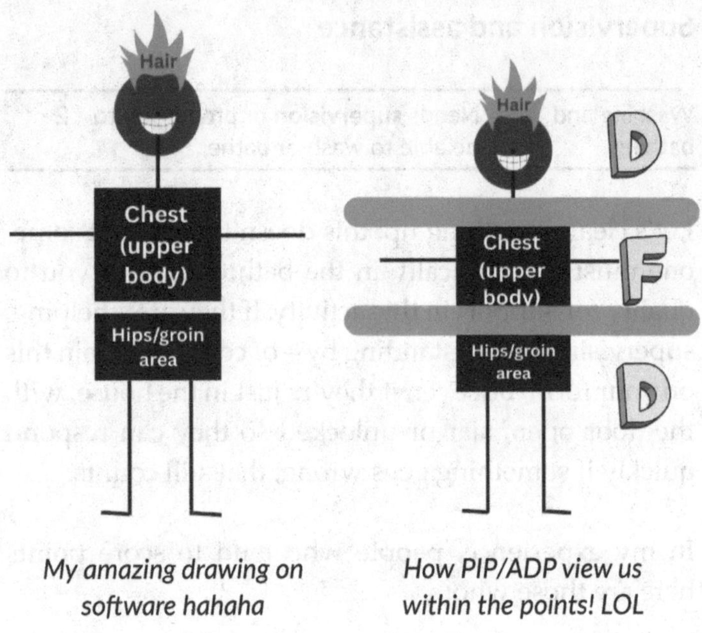

My amazing drawing on software hahaha

How PIP/ADP view us within the points! LOL

Hair and the area below the waist are both covered by descriptor (d):

Washing and bathing	d.	Needs assistance to be able to wash either their hair or body below the waist.	2

This descriptor applies if you need assistance to wash either your hair or any part of your body below the waist. That means help from another person.

Hair: Do you need help washing your hair? If yes, how often? Every time or just on bad days? Why do you need help – is it pain, fatigue, joint issues, dizziness or something else? If you are not washing your hair as often as you would like to but you do not have anyone to help you, explain that too. It still counts.

Describe how you feel while you are washing your hair. Do you get breathless, shaky, overwhelmed? How long does it take? How do you feel afterwards – drained, in pain, needing to lie down?

Below the waist: Feet are so far away! Does someone wash below your waist (whether it's feet, legs or intimate areas) for you? If yes, who helps you? How often? Why do you need help? Is it balance, flexibility, pain, breathlessness, risk of falling?

Between the shoulders and waist: This area – the middle section on my cheery little illustration – might seem oddly specific, but there's a reason for it. The DWP breaks the body down into zones because different movements require different levels of mobility, strength and co-ordination. Odd, but honestly? That level of detail can work in your favour.

Let's talk about the shoulders-to-waist zone, descriptor (f):

Washing and bathing	f. Needs assistance to be able to wash their body between the shoulders and waist.	4

Does someone help wash this area for you? If yes, how often? Why do you need help? Is it pain, stiffness, fatigue, dislocations, weakness or something else? Even if you can wash some parts of your body but not this section, that still counts. Be clear about what you can't do and why.

Transitions: This one's about the transitions – getting in and out of the bath or shower, or onto a seat. It's not about whether you can wash once you're in there, but about whether you can safely get there in the first place.

Washing and bathing	e. Needs assistance to be able to get in or out of a bath or shower.	3

Ask yourself:

- Does someone help you get in or out of the bath or shower?
- Do they help you sit down or stand up from a seat in the bath or shower?
- How often do they help?

- Why do you need that help? (balance, pain, dizziness, weakness, risk of falling)
- How exactly do they help you? Do they steady you, lift your legs, hold your arm, guide you down?

On your form, keep it simple: 'My mum helps me get in and out of the bath.' That's enough for now. At the assessment, they will ask you for more detail if they need it.

Aids and appliances

Washing and bathing	b.	Needs to use an aid or appliance to be able to wash or bathe.	2

This descriptor applies if you need to use aids or appliances to wash or bathe. This means things like a bath seat, grab rails, long-handled sponges or anything that helps you manage safely.

Ask yourself:

- What aids do you use? A stool or seat in the bath or shower? Handles or things you hold on to, to steady yourself? A bath board or transfer bench?
- How often do you use them – every time or just on bad days?

- Why do you need them? Is it pain, balance, fatigue, dizziness, joint instability?

If you can, include a photo of what you use. It helps paint a clearer picture for the assessor. Here is mine:

Also reflect on the following questions and think about your routine:

- On average, how many times a week do you *actually* shower or bathe? If you're not sure, use the diary in the workbook to track it.
- How do you feel afterwards? (exhausted, in pain, shaky, needing to lie down)
- How long does it take you to wash and how long to recover? If it takes twice as long as someone able-bodied, say so.

Here's the most important part: it is critical that you are honest about how often you clean yourself. I have gone months without bathing – I rely on wet wipes. That's not laziness, it's survival. We didn't choose this, and we shouldn't feel guilty for adapting.

Examples of possible aids: Wet room adaptation; modified bath; grab handles or whatever you use to hold on to (eg the sink, towel rail); stool or whatever you sit on; step; tap aid; hair-washing aid; long-handled brush for feet or back; non-slip mats.

> When writing your form, if you won't listen to me, listen to Yoda: 'Copy others, you must not. Your truth, only it will be.'

Real-life examples

Physical conditions and pain-dominated conditions (Group A) example: 'I have a shower once a week. I need a carer to help me get in and out of the shower chair safely. I can wash my arms and upper body myself, but I need help with my hair and below the waist. After I have had a shower, I am always exhausted and need to lie down for an hour to recover.'

Mental health conditions (Group B) example: 'I only shower about every three weeks as there is no point in doing it.'

Evidence suggestions: Photos of your bath or shower setup, showing what you hold on to and any aids – grab rails, shower door, anything you use to stay safe.

With your answer, skip the saga. This isn't *Twilight*, FFS.

Common mistakes

- Feeling too embarrassed to admit how rarely you wash, bath or shower.
- Writing too much and running out of space. If you think you need more space than the form allows: YOU SHALL NOT PASS! Keep it tight. Keep it focused.

Possible scorings

Group A (Physical conditions and pain-dominated conditions)	B, D, E; potentially F in extreme cases
Group B (Mental health conditions)	C
Group C (Neurodivergence)	B or C or possibly (assistance) E or F
Group D (Fatigue-dominated conditions)	B (rarely D or E)

Summary

- This is *only* about washing and bathing (not dressing or grooming).
- They want to know exactly how *you* manage this task. The assessor is looking for detail that is unique to you.
- You score points if you need aids, prompting, supervision or physical help with washing or getting in and out.
- Bathrooms are high risk areas – falls here can be life-changing, so safety is a central part of our claim for many of us.
- Be brutally honest about how often you actually wash, shower or bathe, even if it feels embarrassing.

Using the toilet and managing incontinence

This is about how you manage going to the toilet and if you need help from either a person or an object/aid. It is not just about incontinence and accidents.

Here are the DWP descriptors:

Activity	Descriptors	Points
Managing toilet needs or incontinence	a. Can manage toilet needs or incontinence unaided.	0
	b. Needs to use an aid or appliance to be able to manage toilet needs or incontinence.	2
	c. Needs supervision or prompting to be able to manage toilet needs.	2
	d. Needs assistance to be able to manage toilet needs.	4
	e. Needs assistance to be able to manage incontinence of either bladder or bowel.	6
	f. Needs assistance to be able to manage incontinence of both bladder and bowel.	8

Before we start, let's be clear on what they mean by:

- Bladder: Urine, urination, wee, pee, piddle, 'number 1'
- Bowel: Faeces, faecal matter, stool (not the kind you sit on!), poo, sh*t, dump, crap, diarrhoea (use this word if this is what you experience), excrement, a motion, 'number 2'

There seems to be a big misunderstanding about this activity. Many people seem to think that if they experience incontinence (especially of both bladder *and* bowel), they will automatically score 8 points. That is wrong. In short: if you can manage your incontinence yourself (for example, by using pads), you score 2 points.

The DWP is not interested in whether someone helps you change your bedding or cleans the bathroom after you. It is not part of the scoring system.

What the DWP actually focuses on:

- Using aids and appliances
- Prompting, supervision or assistance – someone reminding you, helping you clean yourself or being present due to risk
- Whether help is for bladder, bowel or both – it's important as there is a big difference in the scoring

Aids and appliances

Managing toilet needs or incontinence	b. Needs to use an aid or appliance to be able to manage toilet needs or incontinence.	2

Do you use aids to help with toileting? If yes, what aids do you use? (pads, bottom wiper, commode, a radiator to pull yourself up off the toilet?) How often do you use them, and why?

Include a photo if possible. Here is mine:

You do not need to be in any photos of evidence you send

Here are some questions to help you describe your experience:

- How long does it take you to recover after going to the toilet?
- How many accidents do you have on average per week? If they come in waves – eg nothing for a week and then three accidents in one

day – average it out. Your workbook should help with this.

- Do accidents leave you more fatigued or has your pain increased?
- Do you have a strategy to try and prevent accidents when you go out?
- If you have diarrhoea, how many times a day does it happen, on average?

Be brutally honest here. If you're embarrassed, that's understandable, but don't let shame cost you points. Use the workbook to track your patterns if you're unsure. The DWP needs to understand the functional impact; not just whether you're coping, but *how* you're coping.

Examples of possible aids: Toilet frame or raised seat; handles / grab rails / radiator / towel rail (any fixed object used to pull yourself up); incontinence pads for clothing and / or bed; bedpan, commode (or any item used to urinate or have a bowel movement); riser for the commode; Bottom Buddy; self-cleaning toilet or bidet (only if medically necessary due to chronic illness – not cultural use); catheters, stoma bags or irrigation kits (used to empty your bladder or bowel).

Prompting

Managing toilet needs or incontinence	c. Needs supervision or prompting to be able to manage toilet needs.	2

Do you need to be reminded, encouraged, prompted or nagged to go to the toilet? (They do *not* mean before you go out, but in normal daily life.)

Ask yourself:

- Do you forget to go until it's too late?
- Do you avoid going due to anxiety, sensory issues or executive dysfunction?
- Does someone have to remind you regularly? How often?
- Do you fail to give yourself enough time to get there (for whatever reason)?

If yes, explain why you need prompting. Is it due to mental health, cognitive impairment, trauma, mobility challenges or neurological conditions?

Supervision and assistance

Managing toilet needs or incontinence	c. Needs **supervision** or prompting to be able to manage toilet needs.	2

Supervision: This does not mean that someone has to be in the bathroom with you. If they are, of course explain this. You might be supervised if you are at risk of seizures, blackouts, balance issues, severe fatigue, disorientation, dementia-related confusion, for example. **Warning:** If you think you will score for supervision in toileting, you will need to evidence the fuck out of it as I very rarely see them award this.

Assistance: Let us move on to consider physical assistance from another person. This is divided across three descriptors:

Managing toilet needs or incontinence	d. Needs assistance to be able to manage toilet needs.	4
	e. Needs assistance to be able to manage incontinence of either bladder or bowel.	6
	f. Needs assistance to be able to manage incontinence of both bladder and bowel.	8

The first one, (d), considers assistance with managing general 'toilet needs' – the actual process of using the toilet. Ask yourself:

- Do you often need help lowering and / or then pulling up your clothes?
- Do you need help cleaning *yourself* afterwards – because twisting, reaching or balancing (or whatever the reason is) is a nightmare?
- Do your legs sometimes give out, or do you get stuck and you need someone to help you get up off the toilet?

If yes, explain it clearly:

- What kind of help do you need?
- How often does it happen?
- Why do you need that help – is it pain, fatigue, weakness, joint instability, dizziness or something else?

This descriptor is about hands-on assistance, not just supervision or prompting, so if someone physically helps you during or after toileting, that's what the DWP needs to know.

We now move on to consider assistance with incontinence:

Managing toilet needs or incontinence	e. Needs assistance to be able to manage incontinence of either bladder or bowel.	6
	f. Needs assistance to be able to manage incontinence of both bladder and bowel.	8

Do you need help cleaning *yourself* after an accident that is either bladder (wee) or bowel (poo)? If so, this is descriptor (e), 6 points.

If you experience *both* bladder *and* bowel incontinence at the same time *and* have assistance with cleaning yourself up, then you might score in descriptor (f), 8 points.

Ask yourself these questions about your accidents:

- When you have an accident, is it:
  - A leak
  - A constant dribble
  - A flood
  - An explosion
  - Poo that escapes when you have wind
  - A tsunami
  - Bed-wetting accident
- Why does it happen?
  - Due to a medical condition?
  - Because you could not get there in time?
  - Because you didn't know your body was going to go?
- Whatever the reason is for *you* is the right answer here.

Then:

- What help do you have? Describe exactly how they help you – do they help you clean yourself, steady you, lift you, adjust your clothing or support your balance?

- Who helps you?
- How do you feel after an accident (physically)?
- How often does this happen? Work out a weekly average so the assessor can see if you score within this descriptor. Note: If you do need help to clean yourself after an accident but it's rare (like once every six months or so), you will not score here.

PRO TIP

Please be aware that you can get pads on prescription. They are not the best but will save you a lot of money.

Stoma bags: I have worked with a number of people who experience leaks from their stoma bags. If you have experienced this, ask yourself:

- How often does it leak?
- Has it ever leaked in public? If yes, what happened? Has it changed how you leave the house or mix with people?
- Why does it leak? Do you have scar tissue where you secure the stoma bag, or is it due to something else?
- Has the stoma nurse suggested extra aids to help stop the leaking?

If the leakage occurs due to scar tissue, I would recommend taking a photo of the scarring to prove you cannot prevent your stoma from leaking. This evidence cannot be denied. It is 100% fact. Great for PIP; crap for you in daily life.

> Thinking of copying what other people have written? Survey says... WRONG! Copying someone else's answers could screw up your claim. Don't risk it.

Real-life examples

Physical conditions (Group A) example: 'I get stuck on the toilet at least once a day as my right leg goes dead. I call my brother and he comes to help me get up. He will stay with me, help me clean up, pull up my trousers, then wait with me until my leg works again.'

Physical conditions (Group A) example: 'I pull myself up off the toilet using the sink because of the arthritis in my right ankle.'

Evidence suggestions:

- Photos of any aids or equipment that you use
- A photo showing your toilet and any aids you use to help you get on/off the toilet (grab rail, radiator, nearby sink)

Think like a Minion when writing – get straight to the banana!

Common mistakes

- Thinking you'll score high just because you experience incontinence; you won't unless someone helps clean *you.*
- Forgetting that using something to get off the toilet (like a radiator or sink) counts as using an aid, and that is points!
- Not explaining how often you have accidents.
- Feeling too embarrassed to describe your actual toileting routine to a stranger, even though that's exactly what the assessor needs to understand.
- Talking about how someone cleans your bathroom or changes the bedding for you – that doesn't count.
- Assuming that because you need help with cleaning yourself after an accident once a month, you will score high in this category. It doesn't count unless it's happening often.

If you think you need more space than is provided on the form to write about your toileting challenges, the sorting hat will put you in Slytherin, where the constipated people go.

Possible scorings

Group A (Physical conditions and pain-dominated conditions)	B, in severe cases E or F
Group B (Mental health conditions)	Severe OCD only, potentially C
Group C (Neurodivergence)	Potentially any descriptor; ignore for ADHD
Group D (Fatigue-dominated conditions)	B

Summary

- This isn't just about incontinence. It's about whether you need aids, prompting, supervision or help to clean yourself up.
- You only score high if you rely on someone to help clean you.
- Struggling with getting on and off the toilet scores, if you need help from a person or rely on aids.
- The DWP doesn't care about help you might have with changing the bedding or bathroom cleaning.

Dressing and undressing

This activity is about how you manage dressing and undressing – getting your clothing on and off. They need to understand any struggles you have, any aids you use, assistance you need and how often you do it. Like with the washing activity, the DWP considers the lower and upper body separately, to better understand your specific challenges.

Here is what the DWP uses:

Activity	Descriptors	Points
Dressing and undressing	a. Can dress and undress unaided.	0
	b. Needs to use an aid or appliance to be able to dress or undress.	2
	c. Needs either – i) prompting to be able to dress, undress or determine appropriate circumstances for remaining clothed; or ii) prompting or assistance to be able to select appropriate clothing.	2
	d. Needs assistance to be able to dress or undress their lower body.	2
	e. Needs assistance to be able to dress or undress their upper body.	4
	f. Cannot dress or undress at all.	8

Even if you are fairly sure that you can do this activity with no issues (descriptor (a), scoring 0 points) or, alternatively, that you 'cannot dress or undress at all' (scoring 8 points), just have a flick through the information below before skipping to the next activity.

As in the other activities, the DWP really focuses on the use of an aid, and/or the need for prompting, supervision and assistance by body area.

Prompting

For this descriptor, prompting is divided into two subcategories:

Dressing and undressing	c. Needs either – i) prompting to be able to dress, undress or determine appropriate circumstances for remaining clothed; or ii) prompting or assistance to be able to select appropriate clothing.	2

The first section (c. i) assesses whether an individual needs reminders or encouragement to change their clothes. Consider the following questions:

- Do you need to be reminded, encouraged, prompted or nagged to change your clothes?

- How often does this occur?
- Why? (eg cognitive, mental health, sensory challenges)

The second considers prompting or assistance needed for the selection of suitable clothing (c. ii). This applies to people (such as those with autism or dementia) who may struggle to choose clothing appropriate for the weather or social situations. Scoring under this category should be very obvious.

Supervision and assistance

Supervision is not considered in this descriptor. Instead, it concentrates on physical assistance, which is divided based on the part of the body affected:

Dressing and undressing	d.	Needs assistance to be able to dress or undress their **lower body**.	2
	e.	Needs assistance to be able to dress or undress their **upper body**.	4

Lower body assistance (d): This refers to the body below the waist, and therefore includes any assistance needed with shoes, socks (evil things!), underpants/knickers, trousers and skirts.

Upper body assistance (e): This is about difficulties with putting clothes on and off the upper body, and therefore includes underwear (bras and vests), tops, jackets, coats, and zips and buttons. To get these points, you will need strong evidence proving that your condition limits your ability to move or manage upper body dressing tasks as they don't like to give these points. If you rely on assistance to put on your tops and could not manage without it, ignore the fact that they do not like to give these points. Tell your truth. If you have stopped changing tops or wearing a bra due to difficulty with getting them on and off, explain this clearly as it's important.

Consider these questions:

- Do you need help getting your clothing and footwear on and off?
- How often do you need this help?
- What help do you need? Be specific: pulling on your shoes and tying the laces; pulling your tops over your head and feeding your left arm through sleeves, for example.
- What prevents you from managing independently? (pain, stiffness, fatigue, co-ordination)

Important note: Many people who need assistance with dressing don't receive it daily, either because they don't want to ask for the help every day (embarrassment) or they simply don't have someone to do this for them, so they stay in the same clothes for several days.

If this applies to you:

- How many days a week do you change your clothes? Don't be embarrassed about this; easier said than done, I know. As I write this, I have been wearing the same clothes, which I sleep in as well, for three days straight, because my physical abilities suck right now.
- Do you change into sleepwear when you go to bed at night? (If yes, well done!)
- Do you avoid putting on clean clothes as they don't 'feel right'? If so, make sure you add this to your form.
- Have your difficulties with getting dressed changed the way you dress? For example, have you stopped wearing socks because you can't reach that far? Stopped bothering with outdoor clothing because it is too difficult to get on and off?
- Who helps you (if anyone)?
- How often do they help you?

Aids and appliances

This activity looks at whether you need aids or appliances to get dressed or undressed.

Dressing and undressing	b. Needs to use an aid or appliance to be able to dress or undress.	2

Do you use aids to help with dressing? Think about aids like a sock puller, a grabber, a stool to bring your foot closer, a button hook, zip pull or dressing stick. If yes:

- What aids do you use?
- How often do you use them?

Include a photo of your aids if possible. Here is an aid I use:

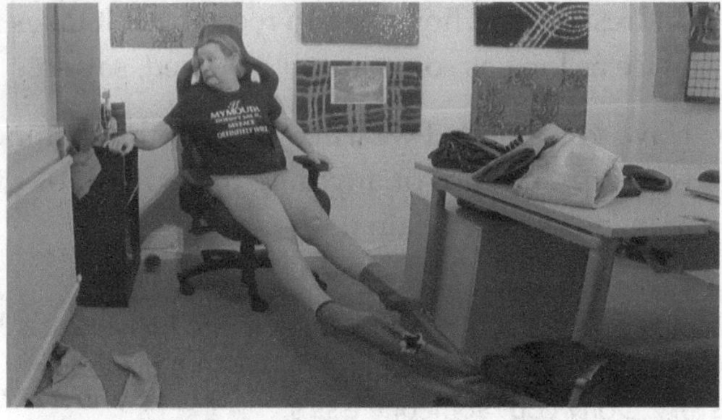

Ollie, my assistance dog, is pulling my jeggings off. I forgot my chair was on wheels, she pulled so hard I started rolling, which is why I look so glamorous! LOL

Many of you, however, might be in the same position that I am: the aids are not suitable. For me, using a sock aid is painful due to hand pain and my fatigue means that I don't have the energy to fuck about with them. If you fit into this category, just be honest about it. A lot of my clients experience this and the DWP will understand this.

Other questions to consider:

- On average, how many times a week do you *actually* change your clothes?
- After dressing or undressing, how do you actually feel, physically and mentally? Consider things like pain, physical exhaustion and mental fatigue.
- How long does it take you to get dressed / undressed, and how long to recover? If it takes twice as long as someone able-bodied, say so.
- Have you stopped wearing fitted clothing, things with zips, buttons or anything that's hard to manage? If so, explain it.

> When you write your form, I want you to imagine you are a superhero. Every superhero has a unique origin story. Don't copy someone else's.

Examples of possible aids: Sock aid; button or zip hook; shoehorn; grabber or reacher; leg lifter; hook or pulling tool for jackets, socks, pants; stool or any seat you have to sit on; Velcro or magnetic fastenings on clothes; or open-back clothing.

Real-life examples

Mental health (Group B) example: 'I only change my clothes every few days as my partner nags me. I just can't get motivated to do it, I feel like there is no point.'

Fatigue (Group D) example: 'I am only able to change my clothes every few days as I do not have the energy to do it more often than that. I don't wear bras, socks or clothing with zips and buttons any more as it's too much for me.'

Evidence suggestions:

- Photos of any aids you use – sock aids, grabbers, stools, rails etc
- A report from a physiotherapist confirming your physical limitations is good evidence if you have one

> Think of Yoda: waffle not. If you think you need to write more than the space allows, this chapter will self-destruct in five seconds.

Common mistakes

- Assuming you'll score just because someone is helping you – if it's only because its quicker and easier, you won't.
- Not being honest enough about how often you actually change your clothes.
- Freezing up in the assessment and not having the confidence to state the facts clearly.

Possible scorings

Group A (Physical conditions and pain-dominated conditions)	B; possibly D or E
Group B (Mental health conditions)	C (i)
Group C (Neurodivergence)	C (i) ADHD C (ii) autism D or E for severe learning disabilities
Group D (Fatigue-dominated conditions)	B only in severe cases; rarely D and E (but I have never seen them give points for D and E)

Summary

- This activity is only about the actual process of getting dressed: selecting appropriate clothing and then putting it on and taking it off.
- You score if you need aids, rely on prompting (either to choose appropriate clothes or to get dressed at all), or need hands-on help with dressing, either partially (with either lower or upper body) or fully.
- Be honest about how often you actually change clothes and what you've stopped wearing (bras, socks, clothing with zips or buttons) because you can't manage them.
- Aids don't need to be official or expensive. If you use the sink to pull yourself off the toilet, the sink is an aid.

7
Daily Living Activities – Communication

This chapter looks at two of the daily living activities assessed in PIP: communicating verbally (talking, listening and understanding), and reading and understanding written information, like making a phone call to understand a letter from the DWP

In this chapter, I'll break down what each activity really means, how it's assessed, and how to describe your reality in a way that makes sense for PIP.

Talking, listening and understanding

This activity is about your ability to speak and understand verbal information *in your first language*. It does not need to be English; whether your first language is Urdu, Polish, BSL or anything else, the DWP only cares about how you communicate in the language that's natural to you.

It's also about your ability to:

- Take in spoken information
- Understand it
- Remember basic information like 'take two tablets daily'
- Respond appropriately

Here are the DWP descriptors:

Activity	Descriptors	Points
Communicating verbally	a. Can express and understand verbal information unaided.	0
	b. Needs to use an aid or appliance to be able to speak or hear.	2
	c. Needs communication support to be able to express or understand complex verbal information.	4
	d. Needs communication support to be able to express or understand basic verbal information.	8
	e. Cannot express or understand verbal information at all even with communication support.	12

If you can do the following in your first language, even if you need to read from a list, you will probably score 0 points:

- Say your name
- Say your date of birth
- Say what conditions you have
- Say what medication you take

That's enough for the DWP to consider you able to 'express and understand verbal information unaided'. The DWP does not care about the following when it comes to this activity:

- Brain fog.
- Anxiety.
- Being bedridden (eg with migraines, fatigue, pain).
- Jaw pain or joint issues that make speaking physically hard. (I have severe arthritis in my jaw; for well over 50% of every day, I cannot talk due to pain and resulting restrictions on my jaw movement. The DWP doesn't care.)

Yes, these things are real. Yes, they affect your life, but they don't count under this activity in PIP. The bulk of you reading this will not score in this activity.

You might now be thinking, 'But Charlie, I can't go to the doctors or see a specialist without my mum – I wouldn't understand what was being said! Surely I score points here?' I get it, but I'm sorry, unless your mum is acting as a *trained* communication support worker – like a translator, signer or someone helping you process verbal information due to cognitive or sensory issues – you won't score here.

Aids and appliances

For the few people who *do* score here:

Communicating verbally	b.	Needs to use an aid or appliance to be able to speak or hear.	2

You *may* score if:

- You use a hearing aid, but only if you cannot communicate at all when you remove the device.
- You rely on a speech valve in a tracheostomy.
- You rely on speech technology to talk (like the late Stephen Hawkins), communication cards or other communication devices.

Examples of possible aids: Speech-generating software or devices, voice amplifiers, text-to-speech apps, hearing aids (under certain circumstances), loop system or sound amplifier, picture aids and communication cards, visual timetables or social stories.

Support and assistance

This activity assesses whether someone can understand and express verbal information if they have trained communication support to do so. It is subdivided across three levels:

Communicating verbally	c.	Needs communication support to be able to express or understand **complex verbal information.**	4
	d.	Needs communication support to be able to express or understand **basic verbal information.**	8
	e.	Cannot express or understand verbal information **at all** even with communication support.	12

It is very hard to score here. I have had non-verbal autistic clients who have not been given the points here. It's shit. If you are a parent or loved one completing this claim for someone who is autistic, please be blunt about their abilities. Spell out exactly what they can and cannot do.

If you're unsure whether you qualify, try this:

Can you answer these questions in your first language?

- Do you have a pet?
- What kind of pet do you have?
- What's their name?

If you can answer these questions, the DWP will probably conclude you can manage to communicate unaided and award you 0 points.

If someone cannot express **simple information** – like their name, what they ate or how they feel – they may score 8 points.

In my experience, the people who would score 12 points here are those who have had a severe stroke with lasting speech/language loss or had a brain injury.

Just be extremely blunt on the form if the person you are doing this for fits into any of these descriptors.

Real-life examples

Do not copy any examples straight onto your form! Always use your own words.

Neurodivergence (Group C) example: 'My daughter has a limited vocabulary; she would not be able to follow directions at all. She can say when she is "hungry", but she will only speak to people she knows and trusts.'

> On the PIP claim form, there are two examples; check them out.

Evidence suggestions:

- Photos of any aids, devices or specialist equipment that you use to communicate
- Audiology assessments (hearing test results)
- Cognitive or neurodevelopmental evaluations (ASD assessment reports)

Common mistakes

- Thinking brain fog, bedridden days or being non-verbal some of the time due to pain or anxiety count here – they don't.
- Assuming the DWP will score this activity fairly – it often doesn't.
- Saying you can't communicate when you can speak and understand basic questions. (This can really screw up your claim.)

Possible scorings

Group A (Physical conditions and pain-dominated conditions)	You won't score here
Group B (Mental health conditions)	You won't score here
Group C (Neurodivergence)	Ignore for ADHD (sorry); autism can be C or sometimes D
Group D (Fatigue-dominated conditions)	You won't score here

Summary

- Most people will score 0 points. If you can give your name and date of birth and read out a list of your medical conditions and medications, in your first language, you won't score here, so save yourself and the DWP time and just state that you can communicate. (They appreciate this.)
- Aids and assistance devices such as hearing aids, communication cards and assistive technology will score 2 points but *only* if you literally can't communicate without them.
- Higher scores (4–12 points) only usually apply to people who have had a severe stroke or brain injury, or who have profound learning or cognitive disabilities or very limited autistic communication.

Reading and understanding signs, symbols and words

This activity is about your ability to read and understand signs, in your first language (whether that's English, Urdu, Polish etc). It's about whether you can do it safely, consistently and reliably (SCAR), and what assistance you need to do so.

Note: If you can only read using Braille, you may be assessed as unable to read or understand signs at all, scoring 8 points.

Here's what the DWP uses:

Activity	Descriptors	Points
Reading and understanding signs, symbols and words	a. Can read and understand basic and complex written information either unaided or using spectacles or contact lenses.	0
	b. Needs to use an aid or appliance, other than spectacles or contact lenses, to be able to read or understand either basic or complex written information.	2
	c. Needs prompting to be able to read or understand complex written information.	2
	d. Needs prompting to be able to read or understand basic written information.	4
	e. Cannot read or understand signs, symbols or words at all.	8

The assessor is looking to understand:

- Can you read basic and complex written information unaided?
- Do you need aids or appliances (other than glasses)?
- Do you need prompting to read or understand important documents?
- Can you read things like:
  - Text messages
  - Facebook posts
  - Google searches
  - Newspapers
  - Letters and forms
- Whether you went to a mainstream school and, if so, whether you had documented need for 1:1 support.
- If you are diagnosed as dyslexic.

Note: If you're reading this book on your own, you score 0 points. If you suffer from severe depression, however, check the 'prompting' bits in case you do actually score.

They do not care or count the following:

- Brain fog
- Anxiety
- Days on which we are bedridden (for whatever reason)

For some reason, their own rule of us being able to do something consistently (over 50% of the time) doesn't count here.

Aids and appliances

Reading and understanding signs, symbols and words	b. Needs to use an aid or appliance, other than spectacles or contact lenses, to be able to read or understand either basic or complex written information.	2

To score here, you must use an aid or appliance that you cannot read without, not something that just makes reading easier for you. Aids only count if they are essential, not optional. Examples include colour overlays, text-to-speech software, magnifiers and screen readers. These must be supported by a formal diagnosis.

Important: Glasses do not count.

Examples of possible aids: Magnifier (handheld or electronic); screen reader software; large-print materials; coloured overlays or filters; text-to-speech software, apps or devices; picture-based communication aids; simplified or symbol-based materials.

Prompting

Reading and understanding signs, symbols and words	c. Needs prompting to be able to read or understand complex written information.	2
	d. Needs prompting to be able to read or understand basic written information.	4

You may score for prompting for complex written information if:

- You suffer from severe depression, autism or cognitive difficulties
- Someone regularly helps you with letters, forms and other paperwork
- You need encouragement, reminders, prompting or support to engage with written information and paperwork

If this applies to you and you do need help, you will potentially score here. Make sure you write about this on your form.

If you are reading this book on behalf of someone else that you have to help, they *would* score here, so be clear and specific about what support they need and why.

Basic written information might mean something like a sign that said 'EXIT' or 'DANGER'. Could the claimant read and understand it, if prompted? If yes, they score in descriptor (d).

Support and assistance

Unable to read (in your first language):

Reading and understanding signs, symbols and words	e. Cannot read or understand signs, symbols or words at all.	8

The final descriptor is for people who:

- Have never learnt to read
- Have severe dyslexia or learning difficulties
- Cannot read or understand any written words or symbols, even with support
- Are totally blind and read Braille

Real-life examples

Neurodivergence (Group C) example: 'My daughter cannot read; she would not understand a sign that said "DANGER".'

Mental health (Group B) example: 'My daughter looks after all my paperwork as I can't cope with it. I can't even open my post.'

> See how little I have written above? That is enough.

Evidence suggestions:

- Photos of any aids you use (overlays, speech software)
- Neurodevelopmental or cognitive assessment reports

Common mistakes

- Thinking brain fog, anxiety or bedridden days counts.
- Thinking they will score fairly.
- Stating you are dyslexic or autistic without having a formal diagnosis and expecting points.

Possible scorings

Group A (Physical conditions and pain-dominated conditions)	Group A	You won't score here
Group B (Mental health conditions)	Group B	Possibly C
Group C (Neurodivergence)	Group C	B C for ADHD C, D or E depending on severity
Group D (Fatigue-dominated conditions)	Group D	Ignore, or be honest but don't expect points.

Summary

- Glasses don't count. Only specialist aids do (like overlays or text-to-speech) and only with a diagnosis.
- Most people will score 0 points, unless you need prompting or aids due to dyslexia, autism or severe depression.
- If you are able to read in your first language, don't waste time here. Just state that you can read. (It helps your claim.)

8

Daily Living Activities – Managing The Wider World

This chapter covers two very different, but equally important, daily living activities: mixing with other people and managing your money. One is about human connection; the other is about financial independence.

Difficulties with social interaction might mean avoiding people altogether, struggling to read social cues or feeling overwhelmed around people you're not comfortable with. Managing money, on the other hand, isn't just about budgeting; it's about understanding your spending and making decisions.

Mixing with other people

This activity is about how you feel when you have to speak to someone you do not feel comfortable with, not just whether you physically can.

What the assessor will really focus on:

- How you feel around people you are not comfortable with
- What thoughts or reactions you experience
- Whether you can:
  - Take a package from the Amazon delivery person
  - Respond to someone at a checkout counter if they spoke to you
  - Go out alone and interact without distress
- If you struggle with this, how you manage to go out
- If you cannot mix with strangers, they want more details and examples of why this is not possible for you

This activity is only for people with mental health, cognitive and learning conditions. Physical conditions do not count, even if they affect your ability to go out. For example, if you have explosive diarrhoea that can't be contained in a pad, as far as PIP are concerned, without a mental health diagnosis as well as the physical condition that causes the incontinence, then you are able to mix with people. Yes, it's bullshit – I'm sorry – but still describe your reality on the form. Even though you might not get the points. You *must* paint a true picture of the reality of your life.

Here's what the DWP uses:

Activity	Descriptors	Points
Engaging with other people face-to-face	a. Can engage with other people unaided.	0
	b. Needs prompting to be able to engage with other people.	2
	c. Needs social support to be able to engage with other people.	4
	d. Cannot engage with other people due to such engagement causing either – i) overwhelming psychological distress to the claimant; or ii) the claimant to exhibit behaviour which would result in a substantial risk of harm to the claimant or another person.	8

If you think you can do this activity with no issues, so you believe you score 0 points, take a moment to flick through the information below before skipping to the next activity, just in case.

Prompting

Engaging with other people face-to-face	b. Needs prompting to be able to engage with other people.	2

Do you need to be reminded, encouraged, prompted or nagged to mix with people? How often does this happen? Why? (Is it anxiety, trauma, depression or something else?)

Assistance and social support

Engaging with other people face-to-face	c. Needs **social support** to be able to engage with other people.	4

Do you *only* mix with strangers when someone you know and trust is with you?

- Why does their presence help?
- What is it about being with someone you trust that enables you to mix with people?
- What happens if they're not available?
- Would you still go out and interact with people?

All of these questions are for you to think about. You do not need to put all of this detail on your form but you will need to be able to explain it at your assessment.

Examples of possible aids: Noise-cancelling headphones (for autism only).

We now move on to the final descriptor in this activity. You may score here if you cannot engage with other people because doing so causes either overwhelming psychological distress or prompts behaviour that poses a substantial risk of harm to yourself or others.

Psychological distress and risk of harm

Content warning: Psychological distress, self-harm and suicidal feelings. Please look after yourself and do not read on if it might trigger you. You can skip this section or return to it later. If things feel overwhelming, please speak to a trusted person, organisation, charity or a medical professional urgently.

Engaging with other people face-to-face	d. Cannot engage with other people due to such engagement causing either – i) **overwhelming psychological distress** to the claimant; or	8

This descriptor applies to people whose mental health conditions are so severe that they rarely leave their home or interact socially. It's not about shyness or discomfort, but about overwhelming phycological distress that is so intense it affects your ability to function 'normally'.

I am not going to give detailed examples or ask probing questions here because this part of the book may already be difficult to read. That's part of the reality and a sign of how invasive PIP is. You're expected to describe how distress shows up in your body, your behaviour and your daily life. Most people have never had to do this, so to figure this out yourself is extremely difficult.

Now let's look at the DWP's need to be able to understand the actual risk of harm that could result from attempting to engage with other people. This descriptor is about behaviour so serious that it could pose 'a substantial risk of harm' to yourself or others.

Engaging with other people face-to-face	d. Cannot engage with other people due to such engagement causing either – ii) the claimant to exhibit behaviour which would result in a substantial risk of harm to the claimant or another person.	8

This might include:

- Shouting, swearing or verbal aggression towards other people
- Throwing things or physical outbursts (including towards another person)
- Physically hurting another person
- Self-harm before, during or after social contact

I am not going to include any more questions here. If this resonates with you, please take a moment. You are not alone. Many people struggle to describe these experiences, especially when shame or fear of judgement gets in the way. It's important you are honest about what happens, but remember you don't ever need to share details of past trauma. It's about current daily life.

I hope this part of the book has helped you without causing you any more distress.

Real-life examples

Mental health (Group B) example: 'I have no motivation. I don't want to go out. If my friend did not nag me, I would not mix with people at all.'

Mental health (Group B) example: 'My OCD is so severe I can't leave my home. It's not safe to be around people as they will contaminate me.'

> Your answers need to be like your fingerprint – recognisably yours. Avoid vague words. Instead, describe what *you* experience.

Evidence suggestions:

- Specialist medical letters that state fact, not hearsay ('She claims…', 'He states…')

- Diagnosis
- Psychiatric assessments
- Crisis team involvement or safeguarding plans

> Your form isn't *War and Peace*. Think more Post-it note than novel.
>
> If you think you need to write more than the space provided on this form: *it's a trap!* Stick to the essentials.

Common mistakes

- Feeling too embarrassed to talk about triggers or risky behaviour.
- Diagnosis and medical records not matching your life. I have worked with a number of people who simply do not go out or who will, very rarely, but only with someone they trust, yet they do not have an appropriate diagnosis, so all their struggles are hidden on paper. Make sure you are getting the help you deserve by being blunt with your GP.
- Not giving clear examples of when social contact went wrong, including how you felt and what happened.

Possible scorings

Group A (Physical conditions and pain-dominated conditions)	Group A	You won't score here
Group B (Mental health conditions)	Group B	Possibly B; C or D for severe avoidance or risk to yourself or others
Group C (Neurodivergence)	Group C	Potentially B or C; rarely D if there's risk of harm to self or others
Group D (Fatigue-dominated conditions)	Group D	You won't score here

Summary

- This section is *only* about how you cope with people you do not know or trust.
- You may score if you need prompting, social support or if mixing with people causes severe distress or risky behaviour.
- Physical illness alone doesn't count here – this descriptor is *only* for mental health, cognitive or learning conditions.

Making budgeting decisions (managing money)

This activity is about whether you understand what money is, how it works and if you need help to manage it. Let's be clear: it is not about you being shit with money. It's not about impulse buys, debt or whether your partner handles the bills because they always have.

Sometimes the assessors won't even ask you about money if it is obvious from your job or how you speak that you are clearly cognitively able.

Here's what the DWP uses to assess us:

Activity	Descriptors	Points
Making budgeting decisions	a. Can manage complex budgeting decisions unaided.	0
	b. Needs prompting or assistance to be able to make complex budgeting decisions.	2
	c. Needs prompting or assistance to be able to make simple budgeting decisions.	4
	d. Cannot make any budgeting decisions at all.	6

Who might score here? The only people who *might* score here are those who have:

- Severe neurodivergence (eg autism, ADHD)
- Severe depression or anxiety
- Cognitive conditions (eg learning disabilities, dementia, brain injury)
- Dyscalculia or similar processing difficulties

If you understand what money is and how to use it, even if you're not great at it, you probably won't score here so feel free to skip this activity.

Prompting

Assistance via prompting is split across two descriptors, depending on whether these are simple or complex budgeting decisions:

Making budgeting decisions	b. Needs prompting or assistance to be able to make **complex budgeting decisions.**	2
	c. Needs prompting or assistance to be able to make **simple budgeting decisions.**	4

An example of a **simple budgeting decision** would be if you can take £20, buy a lunch (sandwich, drink and some crisps), and know that you will get change. If you can do that, you won't score here.

Complex budgeting decisions include things like setting up direct debits, planning monthly bills and managing unexpected costs like car repairs or birthdays.

You might score if:

- You avoid looking at your finances because it's overwhelming
- Someone helps you work out how much money you have to spend and what you can afford
- Someone has to write your shopping list, so you don't go over budget
- You need someone to talk through big purchases, eg gifts, holidays, home maintenance
- You need to talk to someone before you buy things, because you might spend money impulsively
- You're given a set amount of money to manage each week

If this happens regularly, and it's due to your condition (not just preference), you will need to explain how often and why someone helps you, and you should score points in descriptor (b):

Making budgeting decisions	b.	Needs prompting or assistance to be able to make complex budgeting decisions.	2

Parents and carers: They may score under descriptor (c) or (d), depending on severity, if the person you are caring for:

- Does not understand that money is limited and doesn't grow on trees
- Constantly asks for money without considering if you have enough
- Becomes distressed or aggressive when you refuse
- Cannot make decisions about spending, even simple ones like choosing between two items based on cost
- Need full support to manage all financial matters

If this behaviour is frequent and clearly linked to a cognitive or developmental condition (eg autism, learning disability), they should score here.

If you are completing this PIP claim on behalf of someone who does not understand money at all or who is no longer able to manage their finances (perhaps due to dementia or a severe stroke, for example), they should score under descriptor (d):

Making budgeting decisions	d.	Cannot make any budgeting decisions at all.	6

Examples of possible aids: There are no aids that I have found for this activity, due to how they assess us.

Real-life examples

Mental health (Group B) example: 'I can't cope with looking at my money as I know it's a mess. My friend helps me every two weeks. He makes me look at my bank account and he will make sure I have enough to pay the bills. I would not be able to manage without him.'

Neurodivergence (Group C) example: 'My daughter does not understand what money is. I look after all of her finances for her.'

> Treat your claim like an open-book exam. You can look at examples, but if you hand in the same essay as the person next to you, you will both fail. Your response needs to sound like *you*, not a textbook, not a template.

Evidence suggestions:

- Diagnosis letters (eg depression, dementia)
- EHCP reports
- ASD assessment report

> Keep it simple: think TikTok, not *Lord of the Rings*.

Common mistakes

Common mistakes specific to this activity:

- Thinking being crap with money means you score here.
- Not understanding how severe the conditions need to be.
- Assuming you score just because someone else (perhaps your partner or parent) manages your money. (If that's always been the case, it may not count unless it's due to your condition.)

Possible scorings

Group A (Physical conditions and pain-dominated conditions)	You won't score here
Group B (Mental health conditions)	B
Group C (Neurodivergence)	B or C (possibly D); ADHD: typically B
Group D (Fatigue-dominated conditions)	Ignore, or be honest but don't expect points

Summary

- You may score if you don't understand money or need regular help to make budgeting decisions.

- Only people with severe depression, dementia, dyscalculia or fairly severe neurodivergence might score here.
- Most people will not score here, even if they're in debt or crap with money.

9
Mobility Activities – Getting From A To B

This chapter tackles the final assessed activities of the PIP form, the two mobility components: 'Planning and following a journey' and 'Moving around'.

Whether you struggle with anxiety outside the house, physical pain when walking or sensory overload on public transport, this is where you explain how your condition affects your ability to get from A to B. It's not about whether you own a car or use a wheelchair; it's about how safely, consistently and reliably (SCAR) you can travel.

We'll break down what the DWP is *really* asking, how to describe your experiences without minimising them, and what kind of evidence makes your claim stronger. Let's get you moving – on paper, at least.

Planning and following a journey

This activity looks at how your condition affects your ability to get from one place to another outside your home. It's not about physical mobility (that's covered in the next activity). This 'activity is designed for limitations on mobility deriving from mental health, cognitive and sensory impairments,'[6] so if you don't have a condition from one of those categories, you won't score points here, even if you do struggle to go out

Here are the descriptors used by the DWP:

Activity	Descriptors	Points
Planning and following journeys	a. Can plan and follow the route of a journey unaided.	0
	b. Needs prompting to be able to undertake any journey to avoid overwhelming psychological distress to the claimant.	4
	c. Cannot plan the route of a journey.	8
	d. Cannot follow the route of an unfamiliar journey without another person, assistance dog or orientation aid.	10
	e. Cannot undertake any journey because it would cause overwhelming psychological distress to the claimant.	10
	f. Cannot follow the route of a familiar journey without another person, an assistance dog or an orientation aid.	12

6 DWP, 'PIP assessment guide part 2'

What the DWP is trying to figure out is if you can travel safely, consistently and reliably (SCAR). That means:

- Are you able to plan a journey?
- Can you follow a route, familiar or unfamiliar?
- Can you go to the local shop or GP on your own?
- Can you get a taxi or use public transport on your own?
- Do you only ever go out with someone you trust?
- Do you have to get nagged by someone or you won't go out at all?
- How do you feel before, during and after a journey?

If you think you can do this activity with no issues (0 points), just have a flick through the information below before skipping to the next activity.

Prompting

Planning and following journeys	b. Needs **prompting** to be able to undertake any journey to avoid overwhelming psychological distress to the claimant.	4

Ask yourself:

- Do you need to be reminded, encouraged, prompted or nagged to go out? If yes, do you need someone to nag or reassure you before going out?

- How often does this happen?
- Why? What causes the distress – anxiety, sensory overload, panic attacks?

Planning

Planning and following journeys	c. Cannot plan the route of a journey.	8

I am going to be honest with you. I have clients who are autistic who are not able to plan a journey at all, yet they do not get given 8 points. They are tight with the points here.

If you can use Google Maps, you don't score here. If you are not able to plan, you should have great evidence to back up the condition that limits this ability.

Overwhelming psychological distress

Planning and following journeys	e. Cannot undertake any journey because it would cause overwhelming psychological distress to the claimant.	10

This descriptor is for people who are effectively trapped in their homes, or for people for whom going out (even with support) is a horrendous nightmare of an experience. This often applies to people with PTSD, cPTSD, autism or severe anxiety, where the aftermath of going out is as severe and distressing as the event itself.

If you are claiming under this descriptor, they will want to know:

- How it feels to leave your home and be outside (including panic, dissociation, intrusive thoughts you have, sensory overload)
- How often you actually go out (eg once a month with support, only for emergencies)
- How long it takes you to recover afterwards (eg days of shutdown, self-harm, increased pain/ fatigue, decline in mental health)

Following a route

This part of the PIP form looks at whether you can follow a route – either familiar or unfamiliar – and whether you need help to do so. It's not about whether you like going out or whether you prefer company. It's about whether you can follow a route safely, consistently and reliably (SCAR) without support.

Planning and following journeys	d. Cannot follow the route of an **unfamiliar journey** without another person, assistance dog or orientation aid.	10
	f. Cannot follow the route of a **familiar journey** without another person, an assistance dog or an orientation aid.	12

If you can follow a preplanned route and get from A to B independently and without an aid or assistance, you are unlikely to score here.

You may score here if you *always* need one of the following to go out:

- A person you know and trust
- A guide or hearing dog
- An orientation aid, such as:
  - Long or white canes
  - Navigation devices with step-by-step prompts
  - Specialist maps or route cards (speech, written or pictures)
  - Orientation belts or harnesses

The questions to ask yourself are simple:

- Do you *always* need support (from someone you know and trust, a trained dog or an aid), even to

familiar places like the local shop or GP? If yes, you may score under descriptor (f) (12 points).

- Do you always need support when going to an **unfamiliar** place (somewhere new)? If yes, you may score under descriptor (d) (10 points).
- How many times in the past week have you actually been somewhere familiar? Somewhere unfamiliar?
- How do you feel when you go out – before, during and after?
- What would happen if you didn't have your person, dog or aid with you?
- How long does it take you to recover afterwards?

Don't exaggerate or only describe your worst days. Remember: the DWP could check on you and see what you are doing in real life. Be truthful, consistent and specific. Use your workbook to track how often you go out, how you feel and what support you need.

> As you write your claim form, think *Star Wars* – these aren't the words you are looking for, unless they are your own.

Examples of possible aids: Orientation aids (such as a guide cane or tactile maps), hearing dogs/guide dogs, Braille map or large-print route guide, visual or symbol-based route cards, noise-cancelling headphones (to reduce sensory overload during travel).

Real-life example

Mental health (Group B) example: 'I am not able to go out unless my partner is with me; even then, I only go out about once a month to medical appointments. There are too many triggers, I am not safe. I need to stay in my home.'

> Imagine Adam Sandler's voice: 'You're not writing Shakespeare here, buddy!'

Evidence suggestions:

- Photos of any aids you use (eg white cane, orientation device)
- Qualification certificate and ID card for your guide/hearing dog
- Fact-based letters regarding your condition from professionals who treat you, especially psychiatrists or psychologists

Common mistakes

- Thinking physical conditions will score just because your life matches the descriptors.
- Waffling or going off topic in the assessment.

> If you're waffling, abort mission! Go back to base.

Possible scorings

Group A (Physical conditions and pain-dominated conditions)	You won't score here
Group B (Mental health conditions)	B Maybe D Possibly E or F
Group C (Neurodivergence)	B, C, D or F
Group D (Fatigue-dominated conditions)	Ignore, as you won't get the points, but paint the picture of your life on your form

Summary

- This section is only for mental health, neurodivergence, cognitive or severe sensory issues, not physical conditions.
- You may score if you need prompting, can't plan a journey or experience overwhelming psychological distress when going out.
- You may score if you need a person, guide/hearing dog or aid to follow a route.
- The DWP splits familiar vs unfamiliar journeys – be clear which applies to you and why.
- Be specific and honest about how often you go out, who/what you need with you, and how you feel before, during and after.

Moving around

This activity looks deceptively simple: can you walk on flat ground? It is, however, not just about walking – it's all about how far you can do without stopping, feeling worse or suffering afterwards. It's hard to figure this one out and you must have a diagnosed physical condition to score points here.

Here's what the DWP measures:

Activity	Descriptors	Points
Moving around	a. Can stand and then move more than 200 metres, either aided or unaided.	0
	b. Can stand and then move more than 50 metres but no more than 200 metres, either aided or unaided.	4
	c. Can stand and then move unaided more than 20 metres but no more than 50 metres.	8
	d. Can stand and then move using an aid or appliance more than 20 metres but no more than 50 metres.	10
	e. Can stand and then move more than 1 metre but no more than 20 metres, either aided or unaided.	12
	f. Cannot, either aided or unaided – i) stand; or ii) move more than 1 metre.	12

If you think you can do this activity with no issues (scoring 0 points) or you consider yourself totally unable to stand and / or walk at all (scoring maximum points), please triple-check this chapter before filling in the form.

The DWP is only interested in your ability to move around on flat ground. They are not concerned with stairs, slopes and hills, uneven ground or getting around in crap weather conditions. It is also not about what you *could* do, hypothetically, or how far you could walk if there was a flesh-eating zombie after you. This is about what you actually do in your real day-to-day life.

Before we even start talking about how you manage getting around and walking, let's be clear about the distances they are interested in. These are 1 metre, 20 metres, 50 metres and 200 metres.

1 metre:

Moving around	f. Cannot, either aided or unaided – i) stand; or ii) move more than 1 metre.	12

This one is usually pretty clear-cut and there should be plenty of solid medical evidence to confirm this. 1 metre is roughly the length of a guitar, baseball bat or golf club.

1–20 metres:

Moving around	e. Can stand and then move more than 1 metre but no more than 20 metres, either aided or unaided.	12

I am crap with numbers so I have to visualise this in buses. 10 metres is roughly the length of a bus. 20 metres is roughly the length of two buses. The assessors tend to prefer to talk in either metres or bus lengths, so be ready to translate.

20–50 metres (with or without an aid):

Moving around	c. Can stand and then move unaided more than 20 metres but no more than 50 metres.	8
Moving around	d. Can stand and then move using an aid or appliance more than 20 metres but no more than 50 metres.	10

50 metres is roughly the length of five buses or half a football pitch.

50–200 metres:

Moving around	b. Can stand and then move more than 50 metres but no more than 200 metres, either aided or unaided.	4

200 metres is roughly the length of 20 buses or two football pitches.

Over 200 metres:

Moving around	a. Can stand and then move more than 200 metres, either aided or unaided.	0

This is the 'no problem' category, but be careful. If you tick this box, you're saying you can walk that distance safely, consistently and reliably (SCAR), without pain, fatigue or needing to stop.

They are not just interested in how far you can walk. Nope. The DWP also wants to know about the following:

- How long does it take you to walk the distance?
- Do you need to stop and rest? If yes, for how long?
- How do you feel while you are walking and afterwards?

These are the kinds of questions they should ask you in your assessment, so let's break down what they really need to know and how to explain it clearly.

Your body

When you stand up, what happens? How do you feel? When you start walking, what changes in your body? Think about these areas:

- Feet
- Ankles
- Knees
- Hips
- Back
- Upper body
- Any other bit of your body that is affected when you move

Now ask yourself: how do these parts body feel as you walk further? What happens after you stop walking?

Most of you will probably be crap at answering these questions properly. If you are thinking something like, 'It hurts!,' 'It's sore,' 'It's painful,' 'It gets worse,' then that's simply not good enough for our purposes. It's not detailed enough. You must understand how to explain your feelings. For example:

- Which foot?
- Which side?
- What kind of pain? (burning, stabbing, aching)
- Does it build up gradually or hit suddenly?
- Does it stop you in your tracks or just slow you down?

Be detailed and specific. This isn't about exaggerating; it's about accurately describing your reality in a way the PIP assessors will understand.

> Channel your inner David Attenborough: narrate your walking like it's a wildlife documentary.

Now let's turn our attention to energy, fatigue and brain fog. Ask yourself:

- What happens to your fatigue levels as you walk?
- How do you feel the further you walk?
- Does brain fog kick in or get worse when you move around? (Remember: the DWP doesn't officially care about brain fog. I have included this as it affects how you function. I need you to be aware of it so you can explain your challenges more clearly.)

Think of your energy levels as being like a battery. After walking:

- Can you rest and then do the same distance again?
- Or does the battery level drop each time, so as the day goes on, you can do less and less? (My battery is rubbish!)

- Do you pay for it later – more pain, more fatigue, more grumpiness?
- Does your condition mean even a short walk wipes you out for hours?

If this sounds familiar, you're not alone and it's important to say so.

PRO TIP

When it comes to the assessment, they are currently really focused on exactly how *long* it takes you to walk every distance. Reality check: None of us walk around with a stopwatch. Do not get bullied into giving inaccurate guesses here.

What they are trying to find out is how your speed compares to that of an able-bodied person. Is your walking speed the same as everybody else's? Slower? Much slower? An absolute snail's pace?

Use your workbook to figure out where you are honestly likely to score in this activity. Don't worry if you need to monitor yourself over a few days or a week or so to get a clear picture of your reality. That's OK. Most of us never think about our walking abilities like this until PIP forces us to. Take your time, be honest and specific. This is about your real life, not what you could do in a crisis or on a rare occasion.

Aids and appliances

Aids and appliances, are specifically mentioned in descriptors (b), (d), (e) and (f).

PRO TIP

The DWP does not count a wheelchair or mobility scooter as an aid. They need to know how far you can walk without them.

Do you use an aid when moving around? If yes, think about:

- What aids do you use? (stick, crutch, rollator, Zimmer frame etc)
- Do you 'furniture walk' at home – holding on to walls, sofas, counters, chairs etc to get around?
- How often do you use your aid(s) and why?

Be specific. This helps them understand how your condition affects your mobility in real life.

Warning: In late 2024, the DWP quietly changed the wording on some versions of the review form. The new question about aids now asks, 'Do you need to use a *prescribed* aid to help you walk?' When I read this, it scared the crap out of me. Most of us don't get our aids 'prescribed'. We buy them ourselves, often after months (or years) of resisting because we don't want to feel like we are giving up. We are more likely to buy our aids online.

Yes, physios and occupational therapists (OTs) can 'prescribe' aids, but the waits are long and most of us cannot afford to go private. Even if we do get seen by an NHS physio (who can see up to 30 patients per day), they all have budgets that they need to consider before giving out aids so most people are just given exercises (that can make things much worse). This means they just stop going because they don't feel listened to, even though an aid could actually really improve their quality of life.

Until we get clarity on how 'prescribed' will be interpreted, this is what I am advising people:

- Answer the question as if the word 'prescribed' is not there. If you use an aid, say so and explain why.
- If possible, try to get a physio or occupational therapist to prescribe you an aid, even if you are already using one you have purchased yourself.

When Occupational Therapy came to visit me, they gave me a number of aids, but I had already bought myself some. They did not then do me a letter saying, 'She needs this, but already had it, so she actually saved the NHS some money.' That's the gap we're dealing with, and it does worry me. If the government issues new guidance, I will do a proper update on my YouTube channel. I will not do updates based on rumours, only when there's something solid.

Examples of possible aids: Walking stick, Zimmer frame (walking frame), crutches (standard or forearm), walking poles, rollator, prosthetic limb(s), furniture walking (using counters or chairs to steady yourself).

Real-life examples

Physical conditions (Group A) example: 'I cannot walk more than 20 metres before the pain is unbearable. I then have to stop and rest before I can move again. Every time I walk, the arthritic pain gets worse in my right foot.'

Physical conditions and fatigue (Group A/D) example: 'I can normally only walk 30–40 metres as it immediately makes my pain worse, then I stop and rest for a few minutes. I go to the supermarket once a week and I walk just over 50 metres, but after doing that walking, I have to go to bed for the rest of the day.'

> Keep your answers on the form so simple that even Joey Tribbiani from *Friends* would understand them.

Evidence suggestions:

- Photos of any aids or appliances that you use
- Reports or letters from occupational therapists or physiotherapists
- Medical letters that state fact, not he said, she said, they said
- Letters confirming your diagnosis and medications

Common mistakes

- Talking about stairs, slopes and uneven ground – this activity is only about flat ground.
- Thinking wheelchairs or mobility scooters count as aids – they don't for this section.
- Assuming that, as your condition is variable, you cannot answer this and the DWP won't understand. You absolutely can answer, and you must.

> For what your life looks like, you do not need to write more than the space provided for this section!

Think about this answer: 'If it varies – please tell us why.' This is about your average, not your best or worst day, so if your condition fluctuates, explain how and why. You have this book, your workbook and the YouTube channel, so I expect all of you to now know your average walking distances so you can answer these questions clearly and with confidence.

Never, ever tick 'It varies'! Know your averages, as it is critical for your claim. (Otherwise the assessor will have to try and work it out during your assessment.)

Possible scorings

Group A (Physical conditions and pain-dominated conditions)	If pain is only in your upper body, you won't score here. If it's in your lower body, carefully work out which descriptor fits; you could be anywhere on the scale.
Group B (Mental health conditions)	You won't score here.
Group C (Neurodivergence)	You won't score here.
Group D (Fatigue-dominated conditions)	Very hard to get points for fatigue alone. You'll need strong evidence of severity. Check which descriptor you feel matches your averages.

Summary

- The activity is looking at how far you can walk before needing to stop, if walking makes your symptoms worse and how you feel afterwards.

- This is only about walking on flat ground, no stairs, slopes, scooters or wheelchairs.
- Distances are everything: over 200 m, 50–200 m, 20–50 m, 1–20 m, under 1 m.
- It's about what you can do in daily life safely, consistently and reliably (SCAR), not in a one-off 'push yourself' moment.
- Assessors should dig into how far, how long, how fast, how often you stop, and what happens to pain/fatigue before, during and after.
- Keep it simple, know *your* average distances.
- Be warned: PIP assessors may try and trick you into confirming what you *could* do on a good day or as a one-off and then use this to argue you don't need support.

The final bits of the form and next steps

I am not including page numbers here because they change from time to time, so I will use section titles, and we *will* finish your form!

Additional information: Write, 'Please see the evidence document' (or use whatever wording you feel comfortable with, as long as you did actually include the evidence document, of course!).

Additional information continued: Write, 'None'. If you have followed my guidelines, you will (of course) not need to add anything.

Section 4 – What happens next: Put your mobile number here. I advise leaving the 'times they cannot call' section blank unless there are specific times when you absolutely can't speak.

Attending an assessment with a health professional: This bit is important. If you feel comfortable with this, I recommend:

- Asking that they record your assessment. This is following *their* procedure and protects *you*.
- Asking for a phone assessment, but only if travelling or attending in person would worsen your condition or symptoms.
- Requesting a male or female assessor, if that makes you feel safer or more comfortable. They don't mind.
- Asking for an appointment at the time of day that suits your body best, whether that's morning, afternoon or after meds kick in.

Final checklist: Use it! It's genuinely helpful and can catch last-minute errors.

Now, with that, the form is FINISHED! Whooo-fucking-hooo! You did it. Thank goodness!

Now, whatever you do, make sure you:

- Take copies of the entire form (yes, every page).
- Do *not* use their freepost envelope to send it as many mysteriously get 'lost'.
- Send it Signed For, Next Day Delivery – protect yourself with tracking.

You should get a text confirmation when they receive it. After that, expect a wait – it will probably be a couple of months before your assessment.

Rest for a week or so, then start focusing on your assessment.

PART THREE
LIFE AFTER THE CLAIM FORM

10
Evidence And Specialists

In this final part of the book, we move on to life after the claim form. First we concentrate on the next steps: preparing for the assessment and, if necessary, any form of appeal.

In this chapter, we will cover the evidence you must include and why it matters. Evidence is the absolute backbone of your claim. It backs up what you've said on your form. Our goal is simple: we are going to present them with the facts, not grey areas and uncertainties, so the DWP cannot wriggle out of treating you fairly (eventually). To do this, we are going to produce an evidence document that meets tribunal standards. This document is *critical* to your future, so do not skip bits.

Charlie's evidence rules

I am going to outline some very strict 'Charlie Rules'. You can totally ignore me – it's your form – but every rule here exists because I've seen what works (and what backfires) in real-life cases.

Use photos where possible

People retain only about a fraction of written information, so where possible, *show*, don't just tell. Include photos of:

- Aids you use
- Scarring or physical evidence of surgery (eg leaking stoma bags, clubbed feet)
- Badly swollen or disfigured joints
- X-rays or MRI scans (even if snapped on your phone)

Do *not* include photos of:

- Anything involving your genitals or incontinence (diarrhoea etc)
- Someone prompting you
- You using a microwave
- Someone helping you with a task – it'll just look staged and won't help

These types of photos won't strengthen your claim and may even undermine it.

Photo rules that matter:

- Take the photo in your home, so they can see it's not a stock image.
- Do not get rid of your old aids just because you think they look crappy. Old aids show long-term use and this helps your claim.
- Do not over-tidy – keep it real.
- Put all your evidence in one document (eg a Word file, not scattered bits of A4).
- Include your full name and NI number at the bottom of every page.
- Maximum: 13 pages.

If you are thinking: 'WTF Charlie, I have more than 13 hospital letters?,' then go back to the start of the book. Have I taught you nothing? 13 pages is generous! Most clients send 7–9. If you think 13 is unlucky – Great! Send 12 pages. (I snorted with laughter when I wrote that!)

Finally

Check the 'rubbish evidence' section, as this might help you cut the crap. This is about impact, not volume:

- Avoid anything that is over three years old, unless it proves a diagnosis that is not on the GP / NHS app.
- Don't use AI-generated waffle.
- Keep copies of *everything.*
- Remember: this is about protecting you.

Evidence you must include

This section is about what I believe you must submit with your claim. Too many people get tripped up here. Not because they're lying, but because they assume the DWP already knows what's in their medical records or they don't include the right evidence.

You don't need to spend money. You don't need to send 50 pages. You just need clear, targeted proof that backs up what you're saying. That's it. Keep it sharp, keep it relevant.

Proof of your diagnosis/conditions

This is basic but essential. Trust me. I have seen GP records where:

- The condition is not listed.
- The conditions listed are wrong.
- The condition was removed as it 'can't be cured'.

To get your proof of diagnosis:

- Check your GP or NHS app (they all look different, but they should list your conditions).
- Use specialist letters that list your diagnoses.
- Request your GP notes. These are free but be warned: reading them can be upsetting. Do not include the full file (it's often 50+ pages).

Don't spend money on obtaining this evidence, a simple screenshot is fine. Just make sure that the main conditions that affect your daily life are listed.

If you list a condition, they *must* ask you about it in your assessment. We want them to focus on your real needs, not your verruca.

Current prescribed medication

This is another easy one that really matters. It shows that your condition is severe enough to require treatment.

You can get this from:

- Your GP/NHS app
- A repeat prescription slip
- Your pharmacy – ask for a printed list of your current meds (it's quick and free)

Do *not* pay for this evidence.

Evidence of aids

If you use any aids because of your condition, take a photo. I have covered this in more detail elsewhere in the book. Go read that section, if you haven't already.

Optional evidence

This is evidence that you *might* have that should be included:

- A letter proving that someone receives Carer's Allowance to look after you (proving you have a registered carer providing 35+ hours a week of support)
- A specialist's letter stating your condition
- A letter from a medical professional that states helpful facts, such as:
  - 'Patient was out of breath walking into the appointment,
  - 'Unable to walk down corridor unaided'
  - 'Patient required assistance to remove clothing for the examination'
  - 'Patient showed signs of severe fatigue'
  - 'Flexion restricted at 45 degrees'

I need to be clear: do not try and tell a medical professional what to write for your PIP claim. It's so obvious, it looks shit and isn't helpful.

After reading this bit, you might be thinking, this is basic. Yep, it is, but it will help your claim. Use the evidence section of your workbook as you collect what you need so you won't miss anything.

What does count as an aid?

Before we start on this bit, let's get one thing straight.

If you are reading this book because you are lazy as fuck and want to take the piss out of the system designed to support chronically ill people, close the book and jog on. It is not for you, you dickhead. If you are thinking, 'I'll just buy a few aids, take a photo and boom – free money.' No. That's not how this works. You don't get points for owning an aid. Of course not! You get points because your condition means you *need* that aid to complete a task safely, consistently and reliably (SCAR). You cannot fake this.

An aid is anything you use, because of your condition, to help you do a task. It doesn't have to be official or expensive. The DWP even says that 'aids and appliances may be everyday objects'.[7] It could therefore be

7 DWP, 'PIP assessment guide part 2'

something as simple as the sink you hold on to as you get out of the bath. If it assists you in completing an activity, it is an aid.

As I have said before, most of us have to buy the aids we need due to funding pressures and long waits in the NHS. If, however, you've been given an aid by occupational therapist or a medical professional, say so, on your form and in your assessment. Loudly. It shows you've been formally assessed and deemed to need that aid, which puts you in a different category altogether.

For examples of some possible aids by activity, check the previous chapters.

What doesn't count as an aid?

Here's the stuff that *doesn't* count, even if it helps you personally. Don't waste your time listing it, and don't expect points for it: acupressure gear; compression gloves and clothing; sleep apnoea machines (PIP doesn't assess sleep); anything to do with your mouth, like mouth guards; dehumidifiers; air purifiers; ergonomic mouse pads or aids for working at a desk; back scratchers; reading glasses; exercise equipment; massage tools; general-purpose grabbers; headphones and earplugs for noise reduction (unless you are autistic); circulation booster; health monitors (for example, blood pressure machine); and anything bed-related – pillows, blankets, mattresses, sheets, hospital beds, side guards.

Yes, even wheelchairs. They're mobility aids, not aids for daily living activities. Different category.

Do not waste your time or theirs. Focus only on what is relevant.

Rubbish evidence

Tempted to skip this section? Fast track to a failed claim. People send in mountains of irrelevant paperwork and bury the good stuff underneath. I know it's anxiety-driven but it does not help. It just makes it harder for the DWP to see what matters.

Do not include the following:

- **GP letters:** Honestly? Don't pay for one. They're vague, generic and not worth it.
- **Letters from friends and family:** I know one of the forms says you can include them, but I say don't waste your and everyone else's time. Think Judge Judy; think Court of Law: no one cares what your mum says. Of course, she'll say you're struggling. Of course, she'll fight for you (if she is a good mum). DWP will discount it, even if they won't admit that.

- **Evidence of aids that don't count:** See lists for each daily activity for examples of aids that do count.

- **Appointment letters:** FFS, stop sending reams and reams of appointment letters! They do not need to see 20 appointment letters to understand I have psoriatic arthritis; they just need proof of the diagnosis. They don't need appointment letters to confirm I am receiving treatment; they just need to see my medication list. Do not waste time.

- **Leaflets on conditions or medications:** Please, stop doing this. It's insulting, a waste of time and buries the important stuff.

- **Out-of-date evidence:** They don't care that you broke your arm when you were 14 years old and you are now 55; they don't need to know you were diagnosed over 20 years ago with the fucking hiccups! As a guideline: If it's over three years old, don't include it unless it's the only piece of evidence for a long-term, unchanging issue that doesn't show on your GP records as diagnosed.

- **Diaries:** Although this is useful in empowering yourself with invaluable knowledge of your abilities, your limitations and your averages, you don't need to include it as evidence.

Consideration needs to go to evidence from specialists. I have said repeatedly that it needs to be included, and of course that is true, but you do need to use it wisely. Submitting a thick wadge of medical paperwork won't impress the DWP, especially if it doesn't back up what you're claiming, so before you send anything, check it carefully for the following:

- **Evidence that says there is no issue:** Yep, that's right. Sounds obvious, but I have seen people submit all sorts of consultant letters, MRI reports and CT scans reports, but when I read them, what they actually state is 'No issue'. I understand why this happens: these letters are confusing and you're trying to be thorough, but if the report says you're fine, it won't help your claim. Only include evidence that confirms there is a problem.
- **'Hearsay':** If a letter says things like 'She says she's in pain' or 'He reports struggling to get dressed', that's not medical opinion, it's just your words repeated back. The PIP form already asks you to describe your difficulties. You don't need someone else to echo them. What you need is a professional stating their own observations or conclusions.
- **Special note for DLA-to-PIP transitions:** If you're claiming for a young person moving from DLA to PIP, be extra careful. Paediatric specialists often write with hope: 'With training, he should be able to prepare meals.' The DWP reads that as: 'Now they are 16, they can prepare meals.'

> That one sentence can ruin a claim, so check everything before you submit it and make sure it won't be used against you.

You do not need a ton of paperwork to prove you are telling the truth. You just need the right bits. Remember, your medical professionals are not with you at home. They don't know how you get on and off the toilet, how you wash yourself or how you manage meals. I have worked with my specialist for over a decade. He still has no idea I struggle to clean myself after a bowel movement or that I haven't cooked a meal in over 10 years. We've never discussed it.

Working with your GP

Let's talk about something that can quietly sabotage your claim: your GP. Most people assume their GP is the best source of medical evidence, and yes, they matter, but not always in the way you think. The DWP *might* contact your GP during the assessment process, but here's the problem: GPs are not trained to write for PIP. The information they submit can be vague, outdated or just plain wrong. Sometimes it's written by someone who's never met you, or worse, by an administrator with no medical training at all. Don't expect a detailed response. Most of the time, GP surgeries seem to write as little as possible, sometimes fewer than 50 words.

The companies contracted by the DWP send different forms to GP surgeries, but the questions are broadly the same. They ask when you were last seen and then about your diagnosis, symptoms, treatment and how your condition affects your daily life:

- Date when last seen
- Question 1 – Disabling conditions
- Question 2 – History of conditions
- Question 3 – Symptoms and variability
- Question 4 – Relevant clinical findings
- Question 5 – Treatment: current, planned, response and diagnosis
- Question 6 – Effects of the disabling condition(s) on day-to-day life
- Question 7 – History of threatening or violent behaviour
- Question 8 – Patient travel to an assessment centre
- Question 9 – Additional Information

You can read the full list online.[8]

---

8 DWP, 'DWP Medical (factual) reports: A guide to completion' (DWP, 6 August 2025), www.gov.uk/government/publications/dwp-factual-medical-reports-guidance-for-healthcare-professionals/dwp-medical-factual-reports-a-guide-to-completion, accessed 22 October 2025

You can ask your surgery if the DWP has been in contact and request a copy of what was sent, for free. Don't panic if they haven't been contacted. It's not a good or bad sign. Don't fret about this; just keep your focus on what *you* can control.

This book is about PIP, but your health matters more. The point of PIP is to help you stay independent, for as long as possible, but if you can get better treatment and improve your quality of life to the point where you don't even need PIP? That's the real win.

I work with a lot of clients, and I'd guess that about 70% of them take action after our meetings. The most common step? Going back to their GP and saying, 'I'm not OK.' Too often, people are put on a low starting dose of medication, or they're given a generic first-line treatment with no follow-up. When it doesn't work, they stop going back. They think, 'Well, what's the point? It's not working, nothing has changed,' but your GP is not psychic. You have to communicate clearly with them.

For the gatekeepers (AKA receptionists!), here is an example of what you can say when they ask why you want to see a GP: 'I need to see the GP about a medication review as my [condition] has got worse.'

In the appointment, stick to two issues max. You might be thinking: 'Charlie, there's so much wrong with me and it takes so much energy to get there!' Your GP is only human and that's all they can realistically focus on within their time limits.

Be what I call 'PIP Blunt'. Use the same language you'd use on your PIP form. For example:

- 'I am trapped in bed five days a week because of migraines. I have no life.'
- 'I don't leave my house as the pain is so bad.'
- 'I can't even clean myself after a bowel movement because of my shoulder pain.'
- 'Every day I think about ending it. I won't, because of my children, but I don't want to carry on like this. Please can I see a specialist as we have tried so many different meds and nothing has worked.'

This kind of honesty helps your GP understand how serious things are and this helps them move forwards in treatment. Be firm, but polite. Stand your ground.

Working with the specialists

Your GP is a General Practitioner. That means they know a little about a lot, but if you have a specific condition, I firmly believe you need a specialist, someone who's spent years studying your exact issue.

For example, if you have:

- Arthritis: ask for a rheumatologist
- Severe mental health struggles: ask for a psychiatrist (they can prescribe medication your GP can't)
- Chronic migraines: ask for a neurologist who actually specialises in migraine care as those are a fucker to manage

Don't be afraid to request referrals. That's part of their job. Yes, they might need to try a few things first – different meds, CBT etc – but keep pushing.

Content warning: Mental health and suicidal thoughts.

If I'd stayed with my GP and not seen specialists, then I would have taken my own life years ago. I would not have survived without my specialists.

I'm really sorry if anyone finds that upsetting, but I need to be honest with you. My life would not have been worth living. And honestly, that scares me because I see the same pattern in so many people I work with now.

Why am I telling you this? Because it matters. Specialists have spent years, even decades, studying our conditions so they understand them on a level most GPs do not. They can also offer specialised advice and even different treatments and medications.

For example, my specialist's view on my pain relief is very different from that of my GP and this lack of understanding nearly cost me my life and is one of the main reasons I started my YouTube channel. You, too, deserve access to that expertise. You matter, even if this whole shitty process can often seem designed to make you feel like you don't.

Mental health teams and Social Services

Let's talk about two things that scare a lot of people into silence: being sectioned and losing custody of your children.

Being sectioned

You might be thinking: 'But Charlie, if I tell the truth about what is going on in my head, they will take me away and lock me up.' Here's the reality: being sectioned (detained under the Mental Health Act) only happens if you are at serious risk of harming yourself or someone else. If you are taking your medication, speaking calmly and not posing a danger, you are not in that category. You'll stay under the care of your GP or your specialist.

In fact, the community mental health teams can be very helpful. They might check in, offer support or help you access services you didn't know existed. Their job isn't to punish you, it's to keep you safe.

Caring for young children

Another common fear: 'If I admit how bad things are, they will call Social Services and take my children away.' This fear keeps many parents suffering in silence, but a Child Protective Services social worker I met said to ask yourself these questions:

- Are your children clean, fed, loved and safe?
- Do they get to school, do their homework and have food in the house?
- Do you have a backup plan if you are stuck in bed, like a relative who steps in?

If the answer is yes, then Social Services have no grounds to remove your children. In fact, I find that many chronically ill parents go above and beyond, putting their children's needs before their own health every single day.

If you are worried, get a step ahead of it on your PIP form. Say something like, '90% of the time, my mum helps care for my daughter'; 'Four days a week, my children stay with their grandmother as I am stuck in bed due to pain. She's available any time we need her.'

If Social Services do visit:

- Do not be grumpy, let them look around.
- Let them see your child is loved and cared for.

- Ask if they can offer any support – maybe extra childcare so you can rest.
- Or just let them do their job and leave. Then you can breathe again.

Remember: there are children out there who *do* need to be taken into care. That's where Social Workers need to focus. If you're doing your best, asking for help and keeping your child safe, you are not the problem.

Driving licences and the DVLA

Let's tackle one of the most common scare tactics used during PIP assessments: the threat to your driving licence.

I've heard countless stories of assessors saying things like, 'If you feel dizzy, you need to contact the DVLA as you shouldn't be driving if it's this bad.' It's designed to rattle you, and yes, there's a grain of truth in it, but it's often used out of context to intimidate claimants.

Here's the reality: if you are not safe to drive, you shouldn't be driving. That's true for everyone, but most people I talk to with chronic illness are already hyperaware of their limitations. They know when it's a bad day and guess what happens? Yep, they do not drive. Shocking, I know – chronically ill people being responsible. Just look at how much we spend on taxis precisely because we *don't* drive when it's unsafe.

DVLA rules (simplified)

You must inform the DVLA if:

- You lose consciousness or awareness due to your condition
- You lose control of your body (eg seizures or severe neurological symptoms, not bladder or bowel)
- You have significant leg or arm movement restrictions (eg arthritis so severe you cannot turn the steering wheel; leg weakness affects your ability to operate the pedals)
- You've had a heart attack or seizures – there are mandatory driving restrictions after these events

If you are still unsure, check the DVLA medical conditions guidance.[9] It's clear and it's there to protect everyone, not to punish you.

Do not let an assessor bully you. If you're driving safely, within DVLA rules and making responsible decisions based on your health, you're doing the right thing.

9 Gov.uk, 'Check if a health condition affects your driving' (Gov.uk, no date), www.gov.uk/health-conditions-and-driving, accessed 22 October 2025

11
The Assessment

If the PIP form is the warm-up, the assessment is the main event. It's where most claims are won or lost. People often panic about filling in the form (understandably) but then walk into the assessment unprepared. This chapter is here to change that.

We'll break down who the assessors are, what they're trained to do (and not do), what the DWP says *should* happen, and what *actually* happens in real life. If you've ever left an assessment feeling like you were gaslit, rushed or ignored, you're not imagining it, but with the right prep, you can go in with your eyes open and ensure you are heard.

The PIP assessors

The DWP outsources the assessments to several different private companies. These companies hire 'functional assessors', usually registered nurses, paramedics, occupational therapists or physiotherapists. No specialist experience is needed. The job adverts are public: six weeks of training, a starting salary of £38,500–£43,450, and a role that involves reviewing paperwork and conducting assessment face-to-face or by video or telephone.

According to the DWP's 'PIP assessment guide part 1: the assessment process', the assessor's job is 'to assess the overall functional effects of the claimant's health condition or impairment on their everyday life over a 12-month period, using the assessment criteria'.[10]

This is to be assessed according to these criteria, from 'Part 2':

> 'The fact that claimant can complete an activity is not sufficient evidence of ability. HPs [health professionals] must consider:
>
> - Approach – what the claimant needs to do; how they carry out the task; what assistance or aids are required; how long it takes; whether

10 DWP, 'PIP assessment guide part 1: The assessment process' (DWP, 25 November 2024), www.gov.uk/government/publications/personal-independence-payment-assessment-guide-for-assessment-providers/pip-assessment-guide-part-1-the-assessment-process, accessed 24 March 2026

they can do it whenever they need to; and whether it is safe.

- Outcome – whether the activity can be successfully completed and the standard that is achieved.
- Impact – what the effects of reaching the outcome has on the claimant and, where relevant, others; and whether the claimant can repeat the activity within a reasonable period of time and to the same standard (this clearly includes consideration of symptoms such as pain, discomfort, breathlessness, fatigue and anxiety). The impact of completing one activity on the ability to complete others must also be considered.
- Variability – how the claimant's approach and outcomes and level of functional restriction change over time and the impact this has on them.'[11]

I have seen the training materials the DWP use and they are fantastic, but in my experience, assessors are not given the time to follow them properly.

What happens during an assessment?

This is *the most important part* of this process. Many people panic over the form but then are essentially unprepared for the assessment.

11 DWP, 'PIP assessment guide part 2'

The DWP says the assessment should be relaxed and claimant-led: 'The claimant and any companion should feel fully involved … the consultation is a genuine two-way process,'[12] but let's talk about the reality:

- Assessors are only given 45 minutes per appointment. This is bullshit and not fair on the assessor or you.
- By contrast, my clients' assessments last, on average, 2.5 hours.
- If your assessment is over in as little as 20 minutes, you will probably get awarded zero points.
- Assessors are under pressure and often look for your 'weak spot' early on to justify scoring you down (more on this later).

At the start of the assessment, they will normally:

- Introduce themselves and their qualifications
- Explain that this is a PIP assessment
- Tell you that they will ask you lots of questions, and yes, you might have to repeat yourself due to the format of the process
- Tell you to let them know if you need a break

12 DWP, 'PIP assessment guide part 1'

- Reassure you that, if they go quiet, they are just typing
- Ask if you have anyone with you and note their name

Most assessors will ask about your conditions and medication at the beginning of assessment. Personally, I think the better ones leave this to the end, because: a) the information is actually already on the screen in front of them; and b) by the end of a proper assessment, you will be exhausted. Your brain will not be working properly.

Important: The assessor does not decide your points. They write a report which is sent to a DWP case manager. They will review the assessment notes, your form and the submitted evidence and then make a decision.

They never ask the questions in the same order. Every assessor seems to have their own style. There's no set order to the questions, so don't be thrown if it feels a bit all over the place.

Notice periods and appointment timings

You should get at least seven days' notice before your assessment. They seem to try and give people two weeks' notice when they can. The worst I have ever seen is three days. Plan for seven days – anything more is a bonus.

Just a heads-up on the time of your appointment: appointment times can run late:

- Before 11.30 am – might be 30 minutes late
- 12.00–1.30pm – could run 15 minutes to 2 hours late
- 2pm onwards – brace yourself, it might not even happen that day

Yep, that's right. All that stress, waiting by the phone and then sometimes no call at all.

Phone vs face-to-face assessments

Let me be crystal clear: I do not want you to attend a face-to-face assessment unless you can travel and function in unfamiliar environments without triggering increased anxiety, pain or brain fog. These assessments are a setup, unfair and designed to make you fail.

What do I mean by a setup? Everything is being watched and judged. They call it 'informal observation' but it's anything but casual. They assess:

- Your walking distances
- How you open the door

- The seat you choose and how you stand up from it
- Your posture, grooming (including the state of your hair) and clothing
- Your hand gestures and body language when talking
- How you got to the appointment – did you drive, walk, take a taxi?
- How you leave – they might watch you through the CCTV or the window so they can see how well you walk out of the building

Everything is being assessed. It's not paranoia. It's protocol.

Now, I do agree with the need to assess us. The reviews are important for many of us. What I do not accept is that people who are telling the truth, who are genuinely ill and whose lives have been taken over by chronic conditions, are being penalised because they behave differently under pressure. We're getting fucked over as, in the UK, we mask and smile. We say 'I'm fine' when actually we're falling apart, and the system doesn't account for that.

I strongly advise you to protect yourself. Choose the assessment format that reflects your reality. Prepare and don't let them catch you off guard.

What the assessors are really looking for

This section is about strategy. Not trickery or paranoia, but about just understanding what assessors are trained to look for and how you can communicate your reality clearly and confidently.

Assessors aren't just ticking boxes. They're looking for:

- The truth – not perfection or drama, just honesty
- Patterns – how one activity links to another (eg if dressing is hard, I can link this to preparing food too)
- Details unique to you – not generic symptoms but how your condition affects your life
- Consistency – your story of your daily life matching your medical records, evidence and how you manage all of the activities

Many assessors will start by asking about your conditions and how they impact your life. This can tell them a lot about where you might score points. Then they'll move on to your living situation:

- What kind of home do you live in – house, flat, supported accommodation?
- Do you have any aids in your home?

- Do you live alone?
- Do you have pets or children?
- Do you drive, and if so, manual or automatic?

If you're working, they might ask:

- What do you do for a living?
- How many hours do you work?
- Do you work from home or go into the office/ travel to a site?
- Do you have any reasonable adjustments in place? (They should ask this but many don't.)

These might include:

- Flexible start times
- Reduced hours
- Remote working
- Special equipment or software
- Adapted uniform or duties

PRO TIP

These adjustments are possible. Many people think they need to quit their job but often small changes can make work sustainable. Don't assume you're out of options.

'Tell me about a typical day...'

There is also this approach:

- Can you tell me about a typical day for you?
- What are your hobbies?

The question helps assessors understand your routine and your limitations. They might also ask about hobbies. (And yes, watching Netflix, gaming on your phone or bingeing my glamorous YouTube channel all count!) This is not what I call 'PIP Trickery'. These are reasonable questions. Just answer honestly, and don't feel pressured to sound impressive.

By now, you should be familiar with what I think is The Worst Advice Ever: 'Only talk about your worst day.' *Please* don't do this. The DWP's own guidance says, 'A "snapshot" view of the claimant's condition on a particular day at a particular time is not an adequate assessment.'[13] It also notes that 'HPs must also take into consideration the invisible nature of some symptoms such as fatigue and pain which may be less easy to identify and explore though observation of the claimant.'[14]

They are supposed to assess your average, so you need to get a step ahead and know this information about yourself so you can clearly answer their questions.

---

13 DWP, 'PIP assessment guide part 1'

14 DWP, 'PIP assessment guide part 1'

In my experience, able-bodied people often struggle to understand chronic illness, especially invisible illnesses and symptoms. That's not your fault, but it does mean you are responsible for making your reality clear. Don't just assume they'll 'get it'. You will probably need to spell it out. Be blunt if you need to.

Physical examinations and support during your assessment

Let's talk about two things that often get overlooked: functional examinations and whether you should bring someone with you to your assessment.

Functional examinations

I have never had a client be asked to do these as my clients tend to be very poorly, but it's important to know what they are and what your rights are. The DWP call them 'functional examinations', and the assessor might ask you to:

- Stand up
- Bend forward
- Grip with your hands
- Move your arms up, out, back etc

They are only allowed to do this if you consent – you can say no. They are also not allowed to disturb your clothing or underwear.

The idea is that these movements shouldn't cause us harm or more discomfort, but here's the reality: they often do. The assessors from the DWP (and therefore ultimately the decision makers) do not see how much these movements screw us up after we get home. The flare-ups, the exhaustion, the pain spike – that's all invisible to them.

If you're able to move, brilliant – show them. If not, be really clear about your limits. You can say things like:

- 'The pain is already there, before I move.'
- 'If I push through this, it won't ease off, it will get worse.'
- If I do this, my brain fog will get bad and I am scared I won't be able to answer your questions properly.'

Your medical records should back you up. If your condition genuinely limits you, you don't need to prove it through movement. On the other hand, don't refuse to do them just because you're nervous or, worse, think it will help your claim. Only say no if your health actually justifies it.

Should you bring a supporter?

Yes and no: it depends on the person. A good companion can be a lifeline, but the wrong one can make things harder.

Yes, bring someone if they are:

- Calm under pressure
- Organised and focused
- Familiar with PIP and able to prompt or protect you from overtalking
- Fully aware of your daily life and you are comfortable discussing everything in front of them

No, avoid bringing someone if they are:

- Anxious or easily overwhelmed
- Prone to interrupting or dominating the conversation
- Unfamiliar with your condition or the PIP process
- Likely to speak too soon, especially in the first 30 minutes

Sometimes having someone with you can make things worse. If they jump in too early, it can throw off the flow and make the assessor grumpy. Choose wisely.

How to practise for your PIP assessment

Let's start with a reality check. Here's what most people experience during their PIP assessment:

- You will go blank, waffle and forget key points.
- When asked 'why?', you will struggle to explain even the simplest of reasons because they feel too obvious for us.
- Many of us end up crying – it's emotionally intense.
- You will face unexpected questions and curveballs.
- They may zero in on one part of your life – your job, parenting, pets – and use it to challenge your abilities.
- The assessor will usually be polite and conversational.
- You will not have time to read your paperwork; they will engage you in conversation – you shouldn't have to flick through your notes to be able to explain how you put your socks on.

To ensure you are as prepared as possible, you need to practise out loud. Reading silently isn't enough; you need to say and hear your answers. This helps you:

- Build up flow and confidence
- Hear what works and what doesn't

- Reduce the chance of freezing or rambling
- Spot gaps, contradictions or things that need clarifying

Most people think they've practised. They haven't. Practising what you plan to say aloud is non-negotiable.

ROAR: Your prep framework

Understand this: I need you to ROAR! Let's return to our framework:

- Talk about your **Real-life struggles**
- Focus on the **Outcome** you deserve
- Prepare for the **Assessment** with truth bombs. Say what's true for you, even if it's uncomfortable.
- Gather the **Right evidence**

Your assessment isn't just an exam. It's a psychological process designed to spot inconsistencies and test credibility.

Understand the assessor:

- You don't know their mindset, training, biases or what is going on in their personal life.

- Humans only retain a fraction of what they hear. The rest gets filtered through assumptions and keywords.
- Your job is to be clear, consistent and grounded in your reality.

Assessment styles: What to expect and practise

I run mock assessments with a lot of my private clients, adapting my approach based on the client's life and personality. I tend to present a range of different assessor styles, and you can practise them too:

1. The 'Nice' one. I will be nice and ask simple warm-up questions, like:

- How do you prepare a meal?
- How do you get dressed?

Don't be fooled! This is just the opening act.

2. The 'Conditions' one. Most assessors will ask you about your conditions and medication at the start of the assessment. Some will then ask you how your condition feels or how it impacts your life. This provides them with *lots* of information, for example:

- 'I have arthritis in my shoulders: it's a bit sore and I feel tired a lot.' Assessor thinks: 0 points – *I'm* tired, FFS!

- 'I have arthritis in my shoulders: I can't lift my arms above my chest.' Assessor thinks: Dressing – possible points?

I hope a massive light bulb has gone off in your head. This is where clarity matters. Be specific.

3. The 'Jump around' one. They will jump between activities rapidly to confuse you. Stay grounded.

4. The 'Trickery' one. They'll subtly talk you out of points, which is easy to do if we feel embarrassed, like a burden or a failure. I will at some point use this style, but only once I'm sure someone's ready for it. Most fall for it once – never again. Make sure you check my YouTube videos for more help on this style.

5. The 'Targeted' one. They will zoom in on areas they think disprove your claim, such as, if you work, have pets or care for children living at home. Be ready to explain how you manage and what the cost to your physical health is.

6. The 'Take your time' one. This is especially for anxiety, but everyone benefits from making sure they take their time. Practise this: Stop. Think. Only then start to answer. If your brain goes blank, you freeze or start to panic, tell them.

7. The 'Home' one. Expect questions about cleaning, how you manage your home and housekeeping.

8. The 'Hobbies' one. They'll ask about leisure:

- Cuddling your dog
- Pottering in the garden
- Spending time with your grandchildren

From a PIP point of view, these are hobbies and open the door to more probing questions.

9. The 'Distance and time' one. This one seems to wave and wane in popularity with assessors, but fundamentally, they'll try to pin down how far you can walk and for how long. Practise describing this clearly using the information obtained from your workbook exercises.

10. The 'Normal day in your life' one. Some assessors will ask you to walk them through a typical day, from the moment you get up to bedtime. What do you do and when? This is a goldmine for descriptors.

11. The 'Dick' one. I always believe in the military mindset: plan for the worst and hope for the best. In this version, I:

- Apply pressure
- Interrupt people
- Jump all over the place
- Repeatedly say your formal name in a condescending, demeaning or frustrated way

- Use a stern and assertive (maybe even aggressive) tone
- Twist your words

People *love* mastering this version. They know we are building to this, and when we go to start this, they really psych themselves up. When you're ready for this, you're ready for anything.

Assessment practice notes

Where are your practice notes?

If you're working with me, we create them as we go through the practice session. By the time we reach the mock assessments (some of the last things we do), you'll have them in front of you, ready to use. Yes, they will look deceptively basic. You might glance at them and think, 'Is that it?,' but I promise: this works.

This is a Charlie rule: during your actual PIP assessment, only take three sheets of paper in. That's it. You won't have time to flick through folders or look at other documents, and you won't need to. These notes are designed to be fast, functional and focused.

Here's what those three sheets usually include:

1. A summary of your conditions and medication details

2. Your assessment notes, p1
3. Your assessment notes, p2

The assessment notes are laid out in a way that's easy to scan mid-conversation. They're not scripts. They're prompts. They help you stay on track, jog your memory and make sure you hit the key points that matter for PIP.

Let me show you how they're structured. Each line is a shorthand reminder of what you need to say in each activity and to keep you on track. If something is written in block capitals, it's a scoring point. That's your cue to expand, explain and anchor it in your daily reality. You also have reminders (in lower case) of why you manage the activity the way you do – for example, fatigue. You won't believe how many clients go blank when asked, 'Why do you need to sit on a chair?' These prompts eliminate that.

[Your name]'s assessment notes:

Don't forget to inform the assessor that you will be recording the assessment.

Preparing FOOD:

- CHAIR
- fatigue

Eating:

- Husband CUTS food – due to fatigue, NAGS

Manging therapy:

- 15–20 MINS A DAY
- depression

Washing:

- HAIR
- CHAIR

Toilet:

- Accidents, wee PADS, SINK

Getting dressed:

- SOCKS

You won't have time to read anything longer than this, and you shouldn't need to. You are talking about your own life – the routines, the struggles, the adaptations you've made. Obviously you know this. These notes simply help you say it clearly, under pressure.

When the assessor asks open questions – and they will – you'll be able to glance down, see the prompt and respond naturally. That's the goal: to keep you focused on your PIP Gold without freezing, rambling or forgetting the important bits.

Page two of your assessment notes follows the same format, covering the rest of the activities relevant to your claim. It's tailored to you, focusing on your conditions, your routines, your reality.

The approach works. It's simple, strategic and stress-tested. Clients who use it walk into their assessments feeling prepared, not panicked.

After your assessment

At the end, the assessor should always ask if you have anything you want to add. This is your moment. If you forgot something or if you feel something wasn't covered properly, speak up. You will then leave the call / room.

The assessor then uses all the information to select which descriptor fits you for each activity, taking into account whether you can do it safely, to an acceptable standard, consistently and in a reasonable period.[15] Remember that the assessor does not themselves decide your award. They complete the assessment and then write a report. A DWP case manager reviews it and makes the final decision.

With that, we've nailed it! Cue Rocky montage music.

15 Summarised from DWP, 'PIP assessment guide part 2'

12
Real-Life Examples And Case Studies

These case studies are based on real people I've worked with, a mix of wins, losses, partial awards and a range of conditions. I've included physical, mental health and neurodevelopmental examples to reflect the diversity of claimants. Each person's story is unique, but the patterns within the PIP experience are painfully familiar.

If you are one of my clients – past, present or future, I am sending love your way.

Case studies

Here are a few representative case studies, based in reality but modified and adapted for this purpose.

For each, I am just going to state the main condition category that impacts their life, but, like so many of us, their conditions often fit into one or more categories, ie mental health and a physical condition.

When I work with clients, I always give them a code name (which we agree together) so I can remember them more easily. Some of the following code names have been tweaked for the book as they can be quite blunt and potentially offensive for some people. (Although they are hilarious to my clients!)

Code name: The Iceman

Condition type: Physical (Group A)

Support level: Full prep and private practice sessions from the start

Initial outcome: Shockingly low score after assessment (which totally messed with my head). He was articulate, prepared and had done everything right. Mandatory reconsideration brought no change (sadly, that's normal).

Tribunal: The Iceman ended up being called in for a tribunal. We were both exhausted. Months of stress, sleepless nights and endless conversations trying to make sense of it all. We couldn't figure it out. Two days before the tribunal, we discovered the real issue:

his GP records were wildly inaccurate and didn't reflect his daily reality at all.

What changed: We scrambled to challenge the errors and submit urgent last-minute corrections.

Final outcome: A win, but at a lower level than he was clearly entitled to. Still, relief, and we will correct it at review.

Lessons learnt:

- Always include a clear diagnosis and medication list in your evidence to counter GP admin errors.
- Sometimes you need to accept a partial win and plan for improvement at review.
- Even with strong communication skills, bad records can sink your claim.
- This took a full year. Be prepared for the long haul.

Code name: Under Caution

Condition type: Physical (Group A)

Context: Under DWP investigation for alleged fraud.

Initial outcome: DWP demanded over £20,000 back. We met at this crisis point.

Key problem/mistakes: She'd been advised – wrongly! – to describe only her worst days every single time, so when she was seen outside, it looked like fraud. The DWP built over 20 separate allegations based on that flawed narrative – they considered her to be a liar!

What changed: We built a watertight evidence pack, proving every single allegation was bullshit. We focused on the actual descriptors and how she met them, not on defending her character.

Final outcome: Technically, a sort of win. She kept her award but the tribunal reduced her score, and she was not convicted, because she was entitled to PIP.

Lessons learnt:

- Never describe only your worst day. It creates a distorted picture and opens you up to accusations. This client went through hell. I now hammer this point home with every new claimant.
- Your story must reflect your averages, not your extremes.

Code name: The Warrior

Condition type: PTSD / cPTSD (Group B)

Initial outcome: The Warrior did not receive sufficient points to gain an award. This is common among people in this group – many fail initial claims or lose funding at reviews.

Key mistakes: Didn't provide enough detail that was *unique* to them. They avoided describing the 'ugly truth' – the daily impact of trauma on daily current life. They didn't make it personal enough.

What changed: We worked on how to communicate what it feels to be them, but without rehashing traumatic events. We focused on function, not history.

Final outcome: Win! The Warrior won their PIP claim and so, eventually, did every other client in this group.

Lessons learnt:

- You don't have to explain what happened to you; just how it affects you now.
- Telling the truth, however ugly, about daily mental health struggles is crucial.
- Assessors are not trauma specialists. You must spell out the impact clearly, without assuming they'll 'get it' or going into the details of the trauma.

Code name: The Transitioner

Condition type: I was working with the parents of an autistic young person moving from DLA to PIP (Group C).

Initial outcome: The Transitioner, who had been in receipt of higher-rate DLA for most of her life, was initially declined. This is common – cases are often declined or, equally commonly, under-awarded.

Key problem/mistakes: DLA evidence often uses hopeful wording – eg 'With training he should be able to prepare a basic meal on his own.' This could then be interpreted as now they are older and have had training, they can prepare a basic meal. Assessors spoke directly to individuals who masked, gave polite answers or said whatever they thought people wanted to hear, just to end the call.

What changed: I worked with their parents to strip out optimism and focus on real daily limits. We reframed the evidence to reflect current reality, not future goals and removed anything that hindered their claim.

Final outcome: Wins for The Transitioner, and all the other clients like them that I worked with. Some had long battles and it took far longer than it should, and a few did not get the level of funding we know they are entitled to. Many were frustrated by short-term awards (eg three years) despite lifelong conditions.

Lessons learnt:

- PIP is vastly different from DLA. The criteria, tone and expectations are completely different.
- Masking can sabotage a claim.

- Evidence must reflect *now*, not hopes for later.
- Ensure any evidence submitted in a PIP claim application is helpful; don't just recycle the same evidence that was successful in DLA claims as this can cause major issues with PIP.

Code name: The Stubborn Scotsman

Condition type: Mental health (Group B)

Initial outcome: Denied at claim and Mandatory Reconsideration

Key problems/mistakes: His GP records did not reflect the severity of his daily challenges due to his conditions. He struggled to communicate with the assessors, which was *due to his conditions.*

What changed: We built a detailed evidence pack and worked on describing the real-life impact.

Final outcome: Loss at Tribunal – for now. He is continuing to fight, with legal support, at Upper Tribunal, as this is now beyond my level of experience.

What has really pissed me off about this case is that his conditions prove he struggles to communicate what is going on in his head. I feel like they discounted this.

Lessons learnt:

- GP records are critical. Make sure they show your reality by linking with them, and remember, the DWP seem to respond better when your medical records show you are doing everything you can to help yourself.
- For some, getting a solicitor isn't optional, it's necessary.

Final reflections

These stories are real. They're messy, painful and sometimes unfair, but they also show what's possible and what's preventable. The biggest lessons?

- Your evidence must reflect your reality.
- Your communication matters. If you can't describe what life is like for you, get help. Practise. Speak it out loud.
- Your mindset matters. Don't write your form on a good day. Don't let guilt, pride or fear distort your truth.
- Your records matter. If your GP notes don't match your life, fix them.

Successfully submitting a claim for PIP is hard, but completely possible. These case studies prove that, even when the odds feel stacked against you, and they serve as a roadmap for the rest of us. Every misstep, every partial win, every hard-earned success will teach us something.

13
The Claim Outcome

Massive achievement unlocked. What happens next?

Most people don't get the award they deserve, if they even get an award at all. If this is you, I'm sorry. You're not alone and you're not done. This chapter is about what happens next. Not what *should* happen, but what actually does, because the reality is harsh: most people's points don't reflect their life. The decision often feels deeply unfair. It's shit but it isn't personal.

You are not alone and you're not imagining it

If you believe the frantic headlines and the wild misinformation spouted by politicians and keyboard warriors, you'd think claiming PIP was as easy as sighing dramatically in a GP's waiting room. Rub your back once, grimace at the right person or mention you're 'a bit anxious' – and boom! The DWP appears like a genie in a bottle, handing you a wad of cash and the keys to a brand-new Motability BMW. Absolute bollocks!

Anyone who's actually been through the system – or supported someone who has – knows the truth. It's brutal, exhausting, degrading and humiliating. It's designed to make you doubt yourself and give up.

Let's look at the real numbers – not the fantasy ones peddled by tabloids and trolls.

As of 31 July 2025:

- 3.8 million people are currently receiving PIP in England and Wales. That's not a sign of mass fraud, it's a sign of mass need.
- Around 52% of new PIP claims are successful, which means nearly half are rejected. Half!
- 37% received the highest level of award, often after a fight.
- 33–35% of go on to appeal after Mandatory Reconciliation, because they still haven't been listened to.

- 21–48% of appeals are resolved before tribunal, often because the DWP finally offers what should have been awarded months ago.
- Only 5–8% of decisions ever reach tribunal… but of those that do?
- Over 65% are successful. That's right. The tribunal sides with the claimant nearly two-thirds of the time![16]

The system is designed to fail you in the hope you'll give up, but as these numbers show, you *have* to keep going. The odds are absolutely in your favour, but they are damn well going to make you fight for it!

You don't have to do this alone. Let's go.

Your claim outcome letter

I've worked with hundreds of clients, and I can count on one hand the number of times the initial award matched someone's actual needs. Three, to be exact. That's not because people are confused or

16 DWP, 'Personal Independence Payment statistics to July 2025' (DWP, 16 September 2025), www.gov.uk/government/statistics/personal-independence-payment-statistics-to-july-2025/personal-independence-payment-statistics-to-july-2025, accessed 3 November 2025

exaggerating. It's because the system is designed to under-award. It's *not* personal! They hope you'll give up, so when you get your report and it doesn't match your reality, don't worry.

I am really sorry this whole thing is such an awful experience. There should be no need for someone like me. The key thing is to manage your expectations: when your outcome letter arrives, turn straight to the first page. This is where the actual award is listed. Focus only on this. Ignore the rest for now, especially what they write in the 'My Decision' section. This is what the letter will say. Focus only on the decision about the award you have been given. This will give some indication of the points you were awarded. Here is an extract from one of my decision letters:

> *Dear Miss Anderson*
> *Thank you for asking us to look at your Personal Independence Payment (PIP) again.*
> *PIP is made up of two parts: help with daily living needs and help with mobility needs.*
> *I have looked at your PIP and decided:*
>
> - *I can award you the* ***enhanced*** *rate of £89.15 a week to help with your* ***daily living needs****. You can now get this from 21 April 2020 to 2 June 2023.*

- *I can still award you the **enhanced** rate of £62.25 a week to help with your **mobility needs**. You can now get this from 21 April 2020 to 2 June 2023.*

The only thing I want you to focus on is the text in bold: your award and the rate. then check what points you scored in each activity. If they don't match (and it's *very* rare that they do), don't panic.

Warning: Ignore everything else on that page for now, especially what they write in the 'My Decision' section. I cannot express this enough: **do not read it!**

It's templated nonsense that often contradicts your evidence and can seriously spike your anxiety. I've seen it devastate people, and it's not worth it.

Your score

Let's talk numbers. I'm sure of one thing: even if you got the award, chances are the scores themselves will feel off. Maybe wildly off, probably even insultingly off. That's normal.

Based on lots of experience with my clients, here is a table showing the sort of scores that are awarded in the assessor's report, compared with what I felt their actual daily life scored:

Activity	Autism (Group C)		COPD (Group A)		Major depression (Group B)		Arthritis (Group A)		ADHD (Group C)	
	Life	PIP	Life	PIP	Life	PIP	Life	PIP	Life	PIP
Preparing food	4	2	4	2	2	2	8	4	2	0
Eating and drinking	4	0	2	0	4	0	2	2	0	0
Managing your treatment	8	2	4	2	6	1	1	1	2	0
Washing and bathing	2	2	2	2	2	2	3	3	2	0
Using the toilet and managing incontinence	0	0	2	2	0	0	8	0	0	0
Dressing and undressing	2	2	2	2	2	2	4	4	2	0
Talking, listening and speaking	8	2	0	0	2	0	0	0	2	0
Reading	2	0	0	0	2	0	0	0	2	0
Mixing with other people	8	4	4	2	4	4	4	0	4	0
Managing money	4	0	0	0	2	0	2	0	2	0
TOTAL	**42**	**14**	**20**	**12**	**26**	**11**	**32**	**14**	**18**	**0**

If reading this table makes your head swim and your eyes go blind, don't worry! Just trust me: the DWP normally underscores on everything. If you scored zero points, take a breath. I bet it feels like you want to take a sledgehammer to the world right now, but stick with it. You're not the first and, sadly, you won't be the last, but why does it happen? When it does, it usually means one of three things: you did not know how to frame your life in PIP terms, you are not entitled to PIP, or your communication was crap. That's harsh (sorry!) but it's the truth.

The next possibility, and perhaps the most common outcome, is that you did get points but not enough for the right award. Again, this is common. It's shit and it will make you feel like crap to see everything you explained so carefully – making yourself vulnerable and exposed in front of total strangers – about the struggles you face on a daily basis ignored, but it's part of the strategy.

If you've been awarded standard or enhanced rates, and this matches your needs – celebrate! Seriously: shut up, be happy and get on with your life. You've done it!

If you didn't get what you deserve, don't panic. This book has been preparing you for this and I'm right there with you. The claim form is just the beginning. Most people (including me) need to go to the next level, and we'll cover that shortly.

Your award

If you have been awarded PIP, this letter will clarify:

- Your weekly payments
- When you will be paid
- How long your award is for

Reality check: You're probably not getting a lifetime award. I have seen non-verbal autistic clients who do not get them. PIP is usually awarded for 3, 5 or 10 years, with reviews starting around a year before your award ends.

The question is, what happens next? You challenge the decision. You don't give up and let them win, because this isn't personal, it's systemic and we're not done yet. Don't worry, we are ready. Everything in this book has been preparing you for the ultimate battle – the Tribunal – but first, we move to the Mandatory Reconsideration. Let's appeal this!

14
PIP Appeals: Mandatory Reconsideration

You've got your decision. It was wrong. Don't worry, it's normal; even I had to appeal for my PIP claim and my change of circumstances.

This chapter is about appealing your PIP decision. We know the system is a nightmare. We knew exactly how this would likely play out – and it did. If we want to get what we're entitled to, we have to follow procedure. I always prepare my clients by advising them that they will need to appeal, as not getting the right points is a strategy. It's not personal, and the strategy works, as most people lose confidence and give up. Throughout this book, I've been training you and preparing you for tribunal standards, so your Mandatory Reconsideration (MR) is going to be easy to do.

You typically have around a month to appeal, although there are exceptions, which I'll cover later.

The DWP says 'you can apply for mandatory reconsideration if any of the following apply:

- You think the office dealing with your claim has made an error or missed important evidence
- You disagree with the reasons for the decision
- You want to have the decision looked at again'[17]

In reality, this means if you didn't get awarded at all, or if you got a lower rate than you expected (or only one rather than both components).

PRO TIP

Don't worry about how long your award is for. Your priority is getting the funding and then getting it to the right level. I would never advise someone to appeal the length of their award.

A few important things to know about MRs. First, if we're honest, the DWP rarely even bothers reading them properly. *'They do not even read them? Are you sure?'*

Yes, I am 100% sure. I have seen it time and time again. I've submitted MRs with clear evidence – diagnoses,

17 DWP, 'Challenge a benefit decision (mandatory reconsideration)' (DWP, no date), www.gov.uk/mandatory-reconsideration, accessed 31 October 2025

letters, detailed explanations – and they've come back with 'No Change'. I once had a client where the 'decision waffle' in the outcome letter claimed that they were not diagnosed with autism, despite evidence of the diagnosis being clearly included. They clearly had not even looked at the letter.

Want more proof? Another reason I'm sure that they have not read them is that I have often resubmitted the exact same documents at Tribunal stage. No edits, no additional evidence. At MR, the DWP noted 'No Change', but at Tribunal, suddenly the client wins, sometimes via an offer before the hearing. Same evidence. Different outcome. That tells you everything you need to know.

To be clear, MR is the next step. It's nothing more than a box-ticking exercise for most of us, but that doesn't mean it's pointless. It's mandatory, it's part of the process and it sets the stage for the real fight. The odds are very much that you will receive a 'No Change' letter, but we must follow the process even if they aren't. If someone tells you, 'Just say you do not agree with the outcome,' then get away from them! They are talking shit, and we're not going to waste this opportunity.

Second: you do not have to submit your MR within one month, despite what it says on your outcome letter. That's the preferred window, but it's not a hard deadline. You have up to 13 months after the date on the *decision letter* (not the original claim submission date) to request an MR, as long as you have a good reason for the delay, 'for example if you've been in hospital or had a bereavement'.[18] You must explain why your request is late, but your reason could be simply that you needed more time to collect more evidence or were too ill to do it.

If you feel a bit wobbly and want more help, contact me by scanning the QR code below or visiting: https://charlies-journey.co.uk.

Requesting a Mandatory Reconsideration

To kick-start the MR process, you need to contact the benefits office that gave you the decision. You can apply for an MR using the CRMR1 form – call and ask that they post you out a copy or download it yourself.[19] You can't submit it online so if you want to use the form, you'll still need fill it in and post it to the DWP.

18 DWP, 'Challenge a benefit decision'
19 Download form CRM1 from www.gov.uk/government/publications/challenge-a-decision-made-by-the-department-for-work-and-pensions-dwp, accessed 31 October 2025

You can do this by phone, but I would suggest doing it all by writing so there is an evidence trail. Alternatively, you can call them. The contact details will be on your decision letter from DWP. They will ask you for the following details:

- The date of the original benefit decision (the date on your outcome letter)
- Your name
- Your address
- Your date of birth
- NI number

If you call them, they will ask why you are appealing. I recommend simply saying 'the award doesn't match my life. I will explain in my letter.' If they ask you which activities don't match your life, ie preparing food, just list which ones you disagree with. Do not start going into detail like you're on another assessment in case they decide to use anything you've said in this phone call against you in the future.

How to write your Mandatory Reconsideration

I much prefer to keep it simple. I recommend just writing them a letter using your tweaked evidence document. You've already done the hard work. Take your evidence document and only keep the evidence for the areas where you **did not get** the right points. So, for example, if they gave you the correct points for preparing food because you have to sit on a seat in the kitchen, delete the photo that we put in your evidence showing the seat you use in the kitchen. Again, we're only going to keep the evidence in for the areas where you did not score the correct points, also **leave in** the evidence of your medication, your diagnosis and any specialist letters you included – they will need to remain in the evidence document.

At the top of your evidence document, it looks like this but with your info:

Miss Olive Anderson JP ## ## ## #
22 November 2025 Evidence

I want you to add this to the top of the document, as we are going to make your evidence document your MR:

Miss Olive Anderson JP ## ## ## #
22 February 2026 Mandatory Reconsideration

Then I tend to write something like this:

To whom it may concern,
Please can you look at my claim again, as the award I've received does not match my daily life. I did get six points for using an aid in toileting, dressing

and washing. I am appealing preparing food and moving around (awarded 4 points only).

Preparing Food:
Because of my arthritis, I am not able to stand for long periods as the pain increases, so I always have to use a perch chair when I'm in the kitchen.

Moving Around:
Below is evidence of my Zimmer frame that I have to use any time the distance is more than 20 metres, because I have to keep stopping and resting due to pain and fatigue caused by my arthritis in my right knee.

Please can you let me know if you need any further information and contact my GP to confirm my conditions and treatment.

Yours sincerely,
Miss Olive Anderson

Adding new evidence

Important: The only things I want you to add to your now-adjusted evidence document, which is becoming your Mandatory Reconsideration, are:

- Medication changes
- New letters from specialists that you've seen or received since you originally submitted your form
- New diagnoses

Most people won't have new letters or new diagnoses, so don't worry if you don't have them to add.

That's it. The evidence document we worked on earlier in the book was brilliant. Don't start adding unhelpful crap in there. You are only making a minor tweak. We know not giving you the right points is strategy. If you've followed the guidelines in this book, we know that what you put on the form, the evidence you submitted and the way you communicated in your assessment was good enough. We are simply jumping through hoops to get you the right level of funding due to the DWP strategy of not giving out the right points.

Then post your MR by Recorded Delivery to the address at the top of your outcome letter.

Next step? You guessed it: you wait. The average wait for the outcome of your MR Notice is around two months. Don't worry about this delay – any award will be backdated.

If they read it and the decision has changed, congratulations! The process stops here and you celebrate. Sadly, in most cases, the odds are that you'll get a 'No Change' letter. That's OK. It's totally expected – we're just jumping through their hoops at this stage. What we have always been working towards is the Tribunal stage, as that's where real change normally happens.

15
PIP Appeals: The Tribunal

FFS! The DWP *still* got it wrong! You've received your MR outcome and it says 'No Change'. You now have around a month to lodge a tribunal appeal, but what is a tribunal appeal?

An 'appeal' means applying to Her Majesty's Courts and Tribunals Service (HMCTS) for an independent ruling on whether a decision by DWP is correct or not.[20] A tribunal is an independent legal body that reviews benefit decisions. It's not run by the DWP, and it doesn't care what the DWP thinks. A tribunal has its own procedures to follow. It has its own judge

20 HM Courts and Tribunals Service, *SSCS1A: How to appeal against a decision made by the Department for Work and Pensions* (HMCTS, no date), https://assets.publishing.service.gov.uk/media/61ee6f6e8fa8f505985ef48a/sscs1a-eng.pdf, accessed 4 March 2026

and its own doctors and disability specialists. The biggest difference? The tribunal *will* actually read what you submit.

Tribunal submission

To lodge a tribunal appeal, you first need to complete an MR. Don't forget to include everything at the time you lodge it. When you lodge a tribunal appeal, the DWP has 30 days to review your submission and potentially make you an offer or standby their decision. The tribunal wait time is usually four to six months from submission to hearing. Decision letters arrive within two to four weeks after the hearing.

At any point along this process, they might make you an offer before the tribunal. You can accept, or you can decline and proceed to tribunal. These pre-tribunal offers are surprisingly common – around a quarter to a half of all cases.[21] For my clients, over three-quarters of them receive an offer and never have to go to tribunal. The DWP seem to go through phases, and sometimes they don't even look at the submissions. I believe it's because they're so behind. It's currently normal not to be contacted by them in the first 30 days after you submit your tribunal. So don't worry if you don't get an offer here.

21 DWP, 'Personal Independence Payment statistics to July 2025'

There are two types of tribunals:

1. **First-tier Tribunal (Social Security and Child Support):** This is where you are at after doing an MR.
2. **Upper Tribunal:** This is only for appeals on points of law, when you think the First-tier Tribunal made a legal error.

We are just going to concentrate on the First-tier Tribunals. An Upper Tribunal will need legal input and is outside my scope of expertise.

Once your case goes to the tribunal team, you will notice some key differences from your experience with the DWP. The tribunal team follows their own procedures. They read everything that has been submitted (unless you sent in so much crap, it's impossible). They don't lie. They focus on details. They won't let you waffle or go off topic. The judge will consider the views of the doctor and the disability specialist. The hearing is always recorded – you can ask for a copy after the tribunal has taken place, but I think you'll find that the outcome documents are so clear you won't need to ask for the recording.

You have actually been working towards this since you started reading this book. Don't give up, do it right.

Attending a tribunal

You do *not* have to attend your tribunal in person if you do not want to, but I strongly recommend you do if you can. There is a lot of misinformation about this out there. You can choose how to attend: by phone, online or face-to-face (in person). It can even take place via a paper-based review of your case without you being involved at all, but I do not recommend staying out of it. If you can attend, in whatever way possible, please do. As it helps that they can ask you questions. Personally, I prefer online hearings. They're less exhausting, and allow the client to be as rested, focused and as clear-headed as possible. If you're too unwell to attend, that's fine, but if you can, show up. Let them see you.

Beware: Tribunals are scary as fuck. I hate them. Even though I support the process, understand it inside out and know that I am good at it, it still feels like being treated like a criminal. You might even sit in the same waiting area as people attending criminal hearings. I was once searched by security because they thought my drink might contain acid!

The day of your tribunal hearing

You've prepped over the past few months, you've panicked repeatedly and you've probably not slept properly for weeks, but now it's here. You should get at least 14 days' notice of the hearing date. Call if you need to reschedule but try *not* to do this, as it can delay your case by three to six months. Let's walk through what happens during the tribunal, so you're prepared.

Today is about showing up, being heard and letting the panel see the human behind the paperwork.

If you're attending in person:

- You'll arrive at the venue (usually a court or civic building). Allow yourself plenty of time in case of traffic or parking issues.
- You'll check in at reception and be directed to a waiting area. This bit might be a bit grim and is certainly going to unnerve you.
- You might be searched. Stay calm.

If you're attending by phone or video:

- You'll get sent instructions in advance about the system that will be used and how to access it.
- About fifteen minutes before your appointment time, practise logging on to make sure your tech is working, your space is quiet and you've got your notes to hand.

During your hearing:

- Have everything you might need in front of you. Prep like it's a PIP assessment. Note that you won't be allowed any food, but if you need a break, you should ask.
- You will be questioned a lot. Stay focused. Don't waffle. Don't undersell yourself. ROAR!

Who will be there

At the start of the hearing, everyone will be introduced. This will include:

- The tribunal panel (independent of the DWP):
  - A judge
  - A medical professional
  - A disability specialist
- Sometimes there might also be a DWP representative present. They tend to sit quietly and observe. Don't worry about them.
- You (sometimes called 'the appellant') and anybody you have brought with you for support.
- Any interpreters or other specialist communication support that has been agreed and arranged in advance.

- Sometimes there will also be a clerk to do admin.

Tribunals are not public, so there won't be members of the public in the court. They are also designed to be accessible, so the judge won't be in robes or a wig, and you won't have to stand up to speak or use fancy legal language. You don't need to take a lawyer.

What will happen

In my experience, before you go in, someone will come to you and explain what is going to happen. This is normally a clerk. They will check that you've got your paperwork and that you're OK, then they pop back into the room where the tribunal panel are, talk to them for a bit, and then, when the panel are ready, that same person normally comes and collects you to take you into the room.

When you walk into the room, it's scary. There will be at least the judge, the doctor and the disability specialist sitting in a row facing you. They could be sitting around a group of tables, like a normal office setup, or they could be in a raised, elevated seating area, like a posh court – I've seen both different arrangements.

As you walk in, I want you to think to yourself, 'I am telling the fucking truth. I just want to be treated fairly. That's all.' Then breathe. Sit yourself down, get your paperwork out. Take your time.

The hearing will start with the judge introducing the tribunal and the people present. They'll explain the process and what the tribunal is for.

They will then ask you the questions for the area(s) you are appealing. You won't be asked to demonstrate difficulties or be examined, but be prepared to talk everything through. They will be taking notes as you speak, but don't worry; it's normal.

The judge will make sure that both the doctor and the disability specialist ask you questions. They will use their skill base. The judge leads everything, and they will keep you on track. Don't worry if they stop you from talking and then ask you to refocus on key areas. They will at all times remain focused on the key areas in the PIP activities and ask specific questions that link to the descriptors. Just let the judge guide you.

It's going to be intimidating. Everyone must be 'in the zone'. They cannot be fluffy with you. Some of the questions might seem random or irrelevant. That's normal. They're testing to make sure your answers are consistent.

The decision

Tribunal hearings usually last between 30 and 90 minutes. Once you've answered the panel's questions, the panel may take a short break to consider all the evidence and what's been said during the hearing.

They might ask you to wait in the waiting area for a bit while they make their decision – if so, brace yourself, as this will feel like the longest 15 minutes of your life – or it might come by post within a couple of weeks. Sometimes they will just tell you the outcome straight away while you're sat in the tribunal. For a number of my clients, the tribunal was completed within 15 minutes, as they reviewed all of the evidence and they only had to ask one or two questions.

The decision letter will tell you whether your appeal was successful. If you win, it will also explain how your PIP award is changing (including any changes in rate or length of award). If you win, your award should be backdated to your original application date. That means you may be owed a lump sum of arrears.

If you don't win, take a breath. You still have options. You can request a Statement of Reasons and consider appealing to the Upper Tribunal. I don't know anything about Upper Tribunals, so seek legal advice on this. Potentially even more important, try to be open-minded and think, 'Am I really entitled to PIP right now?'

If you've followed my advice from a claim through to Mandatory Reconsideration and then Tribunal, and been told that you are not entitled to PIP at all, you might want to do my PIP entitlement assessment. Triple-check before you put yourself through more months of stress to see if your daily life has been severely impacted enough to be entitled to this funding, as I would not expect you to lose with all the prep we did.

If the answer is yes, you are adamant you're entitled to this, you've checked the points and you know you meet the criteria, then speak to a solicitor and start getting ready for Upper Tribunal.

I'm not going to include an example of a tribunal submission pack in this book, but there is one on my website that you can download for free at https://charlies-journey.co.uk/free-stuff. Tribunals are complex, and to go into the detail required would need a whole other book entirely! I have a video that goes into more detail on my YouTube channel at www.youtube.com/@CharliesJourney, but to give you a basic overview: if you completed your claim form, compiled your evidence, prepared for your assessment, and submitted your Mandatory Reconsideration following all of my guidance, then when it comes to lodging a Tribunal, I simply follow the same procedure that I did in the Mandatory Reconsideration chapter, but instead of using the evidence document, I take the Mandatory Reconsideration, and change it to become the Tribunal submission.

If you have gone through the process of submitting your claim, being assessed and requesting Mandatory Reconsideration before finding me and this book, and you did everything on your own without following my guidance, your Tribunal probably won't be as straightforward as one of my clients or existing members of our community. You now need to try and figure out what went wrong and how to correct it – and that can be quite complicated. If this is you, I recommend you watch the free videos on my YouTube channel for more tips and advice: www.youtube.com/@CharliesJourney.

16
Reporting A Change In Your Circumstances

If you don't have PIP funding, this chapter is not relevant to you. If you do have PIP funding, keep reading.

If you've skipped ahead to this chapter without doing the groundwork, go back. Seriously. You need to know your points, understand your descriptors and have your evidence sorted before this will make sense. There is a reason this chapter is near the end. It's not just admin, it's strategy.

When you contact the DWP to report a change, you're potentially triggering a review. Yes, that means a new form to complete, new evidence and potentially another assessment, and yes, even the possibility of losing your award entirely. If you've followed my advice in this book, that shouldn't happen, unless you've genuinely improved, in which case, congratulations! For most people, this process is stressful, frightening, confusing and full of traps, so let's make it simple.

The DWP only cares about one thing: have your points changed? That's it. Not your diagnosis, not your medication, not your mood last Tuesday. Just your points. Keep this in mind when you think about contacting them. For example, if you receive enhanced rate and the change in your life doesn't affect your entitlement to enhanced, why would you put yourself through hell for no change in funding?

There are some changes you *absolutely* must report as 'these changes can affect your PIP award. Depending on the change, your PIP could go up, go down, stay the same or stop.'[22] These changes are mostly obvious, but please check current guidance if unsure. Changes you must inform them about include:

- Being been told you only have 12 months or less to live. In these heartbreaking circumstances, they are really efficient and they will fast track you to enhanced very quickly and without fuss.

22 DWP, 'PIP: Report a change to your needs or circumstances' (DWP, no date), www.gov.uk/pip/change-of-circumstances, accessed 3 November 2025

- If you're admitted to hospital, a care home, a residential school or prison, you need to tell them.
- If your immigration status changes, or you start/stop receiving EU-linked benefits, it's the same deal.
- If your personal details change – name, address, bank account, doctor – let them know.
- If someone is acting on your behalf and that person changes, tell them.

These are the basics, and they're not up for debate. You don't want to get it wrong: 'You could be taken to court or have to pay a penalty if you give wrong information or do not report a change straight away.'[23]

I think we can agree they are all easy to understand and obvious why we need to keep them informed. However, here's where people panic unnecessarily. You do not need to report things like:

- A new diagnosis, medication changes, short hospital stays, new treatment and hospital appointments
- Counselling, CBT etc
- Using a new aid

23 DWP, 'PIP: Report a change'

- Feeling a bit better for a couple of weeks
- Sleep issues
- Issues with stairs, slopes or uneven ground
- Changes in your mental health team
- Seeing your specialist more/less often
- Financial changes
- GP discharges
- Blue Badge updates
- Job role changes, or loss of job
- Getting a pet or getting pregnant

These things might feel significant to you, and they are, but they don't necessarily affect your points, and that's the only thing the DWP cares about.

Now, there are some changes you *do* need to report. Be warned that reporting these will probably launch a review for you, but you need to protect yourself against fraud allegations. If you go back to work, tell them straight away. If you start driving and previously said you couldn't, you must let them know. If you start college or university, and it changes how you engage with people (for example, you now go out independently without prompting), that's relevant and they must be told.

Let's look at: 'your health professional tells you that your condition will last for a longer or shorter time than you reported before'.[24] Again, I am sticking with the same rule: have your points changed? If you have suddenly been cured, fabulous! Inform them. If not, and your points are the same, I wouldn't contact them.

Going abroad for more than four weeks? Yes, you need to tell them. I am wholeheartedly in agreement with this one. If you are able to go abroad, that's great, but it also tells me a lot about your life, and your PIP score. Your entitlement to PIP also stops if you're out of the country for more than four weeks (unless the travel is specifically to receive medical treatment, which you'll need to prove), so you are legally required to tell them or you could be prosecuted.[25] Less than four weeks? Don't bother them. Holidaying in the UK? They don't care.

Finally, the big one: 'you need more or less help with daily living and mobility tasks'.[26] This is the catch-all clause that covers everything and that will be used if someone makes allegations against you. The DWP will whip out this sentence and use it against you as it's vague and scary, and it's why people panic, over-report and inform them of changes that are not relevant. Here's the truth: if you've done the work in

24 DWP, 'PIP: Report a change'
25 DWP, 'Claiming benefits if you live, move or travel abroad' (DWP, no date), www.gov.uk/claim-benefits-abroad/disability-benefits, accessed 4 November 2025
26 DWP, 'PIP: Report a change'

this book, you will clearly know your averages. You'll know your descriptors. You will know your entitlement, and you'll be able to say with confidence: 'I am entitled to PIP.'

People who understand their claim – who've done the prep, tracked their averages and built a rock-solid case – experience far less 'PIP allegations anxiety'. They don't panic every time something shifts. They don't call the DWP because they had a good week. They know the difference between a blip and a change in points, and that knowledge? That's power, so before you pick up the phone, ask yourself: have my points changed? If not, put the phone down, make a cup of tea and carry on living your life.

17
Reviews

Once you finally have your PIP funding in place, you will have a review with the DWP at intervals. Currently the funding is awarded for 3, 5 or 10 years. The review normally starts 12 months before the funding ends, so two years after receiving the award, you get another form. For some people it can take a year and half to go through the PIP process – claim, Mandatory Reconsideration and Tribunal – then the award is backdated to when they originally logged the claim. Which means that about six months after they finally win… the review form arrives!

I'm not able to write about the review process in detail in this book, but I do want to cover some key areas so that you're aware of them.

Why do they do reviews?

I agree with reviews. I do not agree with putting certain people (non-verbal autistic individuals, individuals with severe degenerative conditions that are not going to improve) through a review. But, overall, I agree with the process. All the DWP wants to know is whether your points have changed since your last review – that's it.

You have done the hard work by actually getting PIP. The review process is nowhere near as bad as the claim process. If you follow my guidance, the review process is painless… OK, not really painless. Even I get stressed and fret about it as well – it's PIP FFS. It messes with our heads. But I promise, the review process is not as bad as what you have already been through.

Different types of review forms

There are currently two types of review forms out there. The old one is laid out like this:

> *Preparing food:*
>
> *Please tell us if anything has changed and approximately when.*
>
> *Please tell us how you manage this activity now, including the use of any aids you need.*
>
> *Please tell us about any changes to the help you need or the help you get from another person.*

Those are all the questions about that activity.

When you have the old form, please **do not** write 'no change'. We used to be able to do that, but nowadays I **do not** advise this. Also, where they ask 'approximately when', you can put a year or a month, rather than the exact day – as none of us write in our diary: 'Today I started using chunky cutlery'!

The new form is laid out very differently. It's more like the forms in Scotland for ADP. I think it's better. It keeps you focused and there is less space for you to write, which is a good thing.

The first Preparing Food question is set out like this:

> *Can you manage this activity with any aids or help? No / Yes – go to Activity Two.*
>
> *Do you need to use an aid, for example, a perching stool, grabbers or adapted cutlery? No / Yes.*
>
> *What aids do you use and how often?*

There are more questions for this activity, but I won't list them all here. They are basically broken down like the scoring system – ie using an aid, prompting, assistance etc.

It does not matter which version of the form you have, they will not treat you any differently. I cannot see a pattern as to why certain people receive a particular form, and I expect the old forms will eventually be phased out.

How to fill in the form

Go and get your award letter, the one that showed you what points you were awarded for each activity. If you have lost this, you can call them and ask them to resend it. I strongly recommend you have this in front of you when you are completing the review form.

Once you have your awarded points in front of you, I want you to have a look at them and ask yourself: 'Is my life still the same? Am I still entitled to these points? Do they match my current life?' If the answer is yes, then completing the review form is simple. Say, for example, in Preparing Food you scored 2 points for using an aid, on the form (whether old or new) you would write:

> *'I **still** have to sit on my chair in the kitchen due to the pain I get in my lower back from my degenerative disc disease.'*

The word 'still' is a very important word on a review form. By adding the word 'still', it shows that in the time since you were awarded PIP you are still using the aid.

If you are not using the aid anymore, or you have started using an aid since you last did a PIP form, then you would write:

> *'I **now** need to sit in the kitchen, as I have declined since my last review because my degenerative disc disease is much worse.'*

In this case, the word 'now' shows that your situation and needs have changed since you were awarded PIP.

On the old-style form, if you can manage the activity without any issues, simply write something like: 'I am able to prepare a basic meal', or simply, 'No issues'.

Evidence for your review

I *always* submit an evidence document when I work with clients on reviews. It is critical that you do this. Go back to the evidence section of this book and follow the advice there. If you already have your evidence document from your original claim, then take that document and update it so you are showing consistency.

The odds are that the person assessing your review will be someone who has never seen your claim or file before. That's why you want to be crystal clear (and blunt, of course) in your answers and evidence. You want the person reviewing you to be able to check your review form and evidence and to clearly understand what your daily life is like and where you stand with your points.

The review assessment

Yes, there is another assessment. Well, sometimes. I want you plan as though you *will* be reassessed – we plan for the worst and hope for the best.

Recently I am seeing a number of clients who are not being reassessed. The DWP are reviewing their forms, their evidence (and potentially past information/GP feedback). Then they are deciding (without talking to them) that they are entitled to the same funding. In these cases, they simply issue a letter clarifying this and confirm the new award length. For some people, getting this letter is a huge relief; for other people, it's a bit more complicated, as their condition(s) have declined so their award should increase. This means they need to start a Mandatory Reconsideration (if they want to do this).

The review assessment is not like a claim assessment. They don't ask you what type of property you live in, whether you have pets etc. They are interested in how you manage now and whether there have been any changes since your original award. With my clients, a claim assessment takes on average 2.5 hours.

On average, a review assessment takes 45 minutes. It truly is a different experience.

In summary

If you're reading this book because you have a review, you need to start at the beginning and make sure you understand PIP, your life and how to clearly communicate your norm in a way that works for PIP.

Remember, I follow the same approach for claims and reviews. Keep it simple, be blunt and state facts about your current daily life following the guidelines in this book, and you will be doing everything you can to protect yourself.

A Final Note From Me: This Is Just The Beginning

This book is about helping you win a fair level of PIP funding, but our true goal is improving your quality of life. PIP will help you, but don't stop there. Don't accept a quality of life that sucks. Here are some of the things that have helped me.

The best things I've spent my PIP money on, and that have changed my life, include a housekeeper (my number one recommendation!), a posh bath chair, an automatic lawnmower, a robot hoover, transport, physio, a cheap, second-hand, automatic car, takeaways, and much more. My assistance dog has been absolutely life-changing, and I can't imagine life without her now. I would not have been able to afford to get her and do the training courses and qualifications without my PIP funding.

Treatments. Check in with your pain and fatigue levels. Be honest and real with yourself. If you are frequently scoring a 5+ on the pain and/or fatigue score, get help. Try all the treatments you can. Be open-minded and explore all the options available out there. Remember, you are unique, so you have to figure out what works for your body.

Movement, not 'exercise' – I think 'movement' is a better term. For those of us with chronic illness, even lifting our arms a few times can be a workout. For me, even three reps of lifting my arms up to chest height gets me sweating! We do need to try and move when we can, because we become frail quickly if we stop. Whether you're working with a physio or moving on your own, remember my rule: no big pain or symptom spikes at the time or afterwards. Some muscle soreness is fine, good in fact, but major pain afterwards? Nope. Be careful and do what works for your body.

Home tweaks. Look at your home. Can you do anything to make life easier for yourself? I keep my clothes next to my bed, so I don't waste energy walking to get dressed. I make everything about my life as efficient as possible, so I can use what little energy I have for nice things, like chatting to a friend or having reduced brain 'frog' so I can watch *Taskmaster*.

Pacing is the hardest thing I've ever learnt to do. It's harder than the PIP form, harder than asking for help, harder than accepting that my life is different now.

Done right, though, it's also the most powerful. It's the most positively life-changing thing I have ever done. Good pacing means doing the same amount daily, even when you feel 'better'. It means resisting the urge to push through and crash. Over time, it means slowly, steadily reclaiming parts of your life.

Asking for help. This part sucks. It can feel humiliating. Worse is when you do ask and people don't help. Asking for help isn't a luxury or even a sign of weakness, it's survival. If you have plenty of willing family around you, you are lucky. Many of us have to rely on paid support, but this quickly gets expensive. If you can't pay, think about skill trades. If you're surrounded by people who drag you down, start choosing your circle more carefully. I heard in a podcast that you need the right people around you who lift you up, who help you, not people who drain you. It's hard to do, but really does make a positive difference in our lives. You deserve support, not sabotage.

Fight for yourself. PIP is one part of that fight. You have to do the rest. You're allowed to adapt. You're allowed to thrive. You're allowed to want more. I know you're stronger than you could ever imagine, so use your stubbornness to fight for yourself, adjust and try.

It's different. Yes, your life will be different than you thought it would be. This is a new chapter. Around one in four of us in the UK is disabled,[27] and every single one of us matters and is valued. You are not alone. I'll keep making videos so we can keep growing our community and sharing our experiences. Join the newsletter, watch YouTube, follow on Instagram. Together, we'll keep pushing for the quality of life we deserve. Find me at https://charlies-journey.co.uk.

This is just the beginning.

27 DWP, 'The employment of disabled people 2025' (DWP, 4 November 2025), www.gov.uk/government/statistics/the-employment-of-disabled-people-2025/the-employment-of-disabled-people-2025, accessed 5 November 2025

Acknowledgements

Thank you, Mum and Lauren, I would be f*cked without you.

Thank you also to everyone who supports my newsletter and YouTube channel. Special thanks to those who donated towards the publishing costs of this book:

Alison
Annette
Annmarie
Barry
Caroline
Dave
David
Debbie
Denise
Donal
Ed N
Emma
Francesca
Hagar
Home is where the heart is
Jane
Joanne
JoJo
Ju
Julia
Julie C
Julie S
Justine

Katie H
Katie R
Ken
Lisa
Lyn
Lyn H
Lynne
Maria
Maria
Marie
Melissa
Morgan
Muldoon
Neil
Richard
Rose
Sam
Sarah
Sasha
Shanie
Shapour
Sharon
Sheila
Squidgy
SunWater
TMF
Tracey
Victor
Xavier

The Author

Charlie Anderson is a straight-talking advocate for people living with chronic illness. After developing severe psoriatic arthritis in her late twenties, she went from running multimillion-pound logistics contracts and working on international development projects in Africa, to losing her career, her independence and a decade of her life to pain, fatigue and horrendous side effects from 'treatment'.

That brutal personal experience collided with a scarring benefits system. When Charlie applied for PIP herself, she found the process degrading, confusing and stacked against the people who genuinely needed help. She fought her way through it, won her award and quickly realised most people don't have the confidence, language or inside knowledge to do the same.

Charlie launched her YouTube channel to try to help people going through the same pain and suffering she was living every minute of the day, and to hopefully reduce the time others spent in what she calls 'survival mode'. Her 'cut the crap' guides to PIP have reached hundreds of thousands of people and built a community of claimants who feel less alone and more capable. From there, she created a consultancy to support clients one-to-one, developing tools, strategies and training that consistently help people secure the funding they're entitled to.

Unlike many so-called experts, Charlie isn't a medical professional or lawyer. She's lived the reality of chronic illness every day for nearly two decades, balancing pain, fatigue and brain fog while learning how to beat a system designed to say 'no'. That lived experience, combined with her professional background in leadership, training and problem-solving, makes her uniquely effective at cutting through the noise and focusing on what really matters.

Charlie's mission is simple: to make sure no one has to face the PIP process feeling powerless. Through her book, videos and practical resources, she shows people how to tell the truth about their lives clearly, bluntly and in a way the system can't ignore.

https://charlies-journey.co.uk

www.facebook.com/p/Charlies-Journey-PIP-61557187996575

www.linkedin.com/in/charlotte-charlie-anderson-0682a439

@charli3sjourn3y

www.ingramcontent.com/pod-product-compliance
Lightning Source LLC
LaVergne TN
LVHW030917080826
845145LV00013B/2937